Your Toolbox to

UNLEASH YOUR S⚥PERPOWERS

Korra O'Neill
Tara Lynn Steele

Your Toolbox to Unleash Your Superpowers
Copyright - 2022 by Tara Lynn Steele

All rights reserved. No part of this book may be reproduced in any form or by any electronic or mechanical means, including information storage and retrieval systems, without permission in writing from the author. All rights reserved. No part of this publication may be reproduced, distributed, or transmitted in any form or by any means, including photocopying, recording, or other electronic or mechanical methods, without the prior written permission of the publisher or author, except in the case of brief quotations embodied in critical reviews and certain other noncommercial uses permitted by copyright law. For permission requests, email the publisher or author at:
hello@unleash-your-superpowers.com

The content of this book is for general instruction only. Each person's physical, emotional, and spiritual condition is unique. The instruction in this book is not intended to replace or interrupt the reader's relationship with a physician or other professional. Please consult your doctor for matters pertaining to your specific health and diet.

To contact the author, visit: www.unleash-your-superpowers.com

Printed in the United States of America.

Your Toolbox to
UNLEASH YOUR S♈PERPOWERS

Why?
To personally empower menstruating humans so that they can unleash their superpowers and reach their human hardware's peak performance.

Who?
You lovely, whether you flow freely, take hormones that stop your period, get a wonky flow, or simply don't know where your period went, this book is for you.

What?
Your toolbox for harnessing your hardware's biology, harmonizing your hormones, and most of all unleashing your superpowers!

Enjoy!
Korra & TL

website: www.unleash-your-superpowers.com
Instagram: @unleashyoursuperpowers
email: hello@unleash-your-superpowers.com

Dedication

Contents

Introduction .... **.8**

1: Your Toolbox Tutorial **14**
    Your Uterus
    Your Ovaries
    Biologically Male & Female
    The Two Halves of your Cycle
    TL;DR

2: Menstruation (The Event) **22**
    Report Card
    Intuition
    We're Strong AF
    Bleeding
    Using These Superpowers
    TL;DR

3: Follicular Phase (Pure) **42**
    Stress? What Stress?
    Mood & Resiliency
    Heightened Creativity, Planning, and Problem-Solving
    Micronutrient Absorption
    Heightened Immunity
    Technique Retention
    Using These Superpowers
    TL;DR

4: Ovulation (The Event) **56**
    Attractive
    Sociability
    Orgasms
    Appetite
    Injury Prevention
    Follicular+
    Risk-Taking
    Ask the World for What You Want
    Tracking
    TL;DR

5: Luteal Phase 70
Taskmaster
Stamina
Using These Superpowers
Support
TL;DR

6: Food 80
One of the Things That Makes Us So Super
Immunity
Microbiome Care
Food For Menstruation
Supportive Period Foods
Where Period Meets Follicular
Supportive Foods For the Pure Follicular Phase
The Ovulating Body
Supportive Foods For Ovulation
Where Our Biology Diverges from Diet ....
   Industry
Supportive Foods For the Luteal Phase
Food is Nourishment
TL;DR

7: Breathe 106
8 Ways to Make Breath Work Work For You
TL;DR

8: Movement as Medicine 118
Wiggles For Your Period
Wiggles For Your Follicular Phase
Wiggles For Ovulation
Wiggles For Your Luteal Phase
TL;DR

9: Mental Gymnastics 126
TL;DR

10: Birth Control and Hormone Replacement Therapy 132

    The Barely Audible Infradian Rythym
    Effects Birth Controls Have on our Human
      Hardware
    How to Turn Your Experience Into Data
    HRT & a Note From Our Contributors
    Our Journeys
    TL;DR

11: Imbalanced Hormones and Health Conditions 156
    Small Imbalances
    PCOS
    Endometriosis
    PMDD
    TL;DR

12: Now go out and live your Superpowered life! 170

Recipes 172
Cheat Sheet 183
Resources 184
Thank You 188
Bibliography 190
About The Authors 198

Introduction

Have you ever felt like you are living the dream & winning at life one week, then the next you are trudging through the mud to do even the most basic tasks? Have you ever cried into your coffee about not having the energy to keep up with the hustle that "everyone else" seems to exude daily? Well, guess what?! You aren't alone. This book is a guide for the menstruating human to discover their hidden power and repair the most important relationship we all have in our lives: the relationship we have with ourselves!

Every day we are blasted with the concepts of *DO, output, deliver!* We are conditioned to believe that our world is a singular path we must follow, and that path is a LINEAR path. But, it turns out, there's more than one path: the linear path was created for cis-male biology---but you're a menstruating human! You have the option to walk the *cyclical* path, and you aren't alone . . . a little over one-third of the population is right there with you, struggling to be the square peg in a round hole.

Before we jump the gun, let's chat about how we began our path, and, in turn, discovered all this cyclical stuff. During the late fall of 2019 (about 20 cycles ago), in a 2nd-floor walk-up in Harlem, Korra O'Neill stopped a conversation between two personal trainers in order to say:

"But that workout wouldn't work for most women *all the time*. Our bodies and brains are different from week to week."

In afterthought she added, "It's why they don't study us."

She was met with blank looks, so she continued: "Almost all of the science, including fitness science, is based on cis-male and post-menopausal biology. They don't really study menstruating humans. In most entry-level personal trainer books, we get relegated to an asterisk at the bottom that says 'increase reps and lower the weight'---which is BS!"

TL Steele declared, "I'm tired of being an asterisk!"

And that, folks, is what this book is for---to put menstruating humans at the front and center. For many of you reading this book, it may be the first time in your life that you are getting the special attention your glorious body deserves---*without* talking about how it's equipped to make a baby. And granted, we will touch on that topic---the baby-building---but only very briefly because there is just so much else going on with our human hardware and *so much more* to be gained than pure reproduction. And the best news is that we can reap these benefits *every dang day*.

We hope to be supportive and enlightening guides through these next 170-some odd pages. However, we acknowledge that we, Coach Korra and Coach TL, are not perfect. We are humans on this earth, learning and growing each day, just as all of you are. Coach Korra is an

Integrative Nutrition Health Coach, and at the time of this book-writing, a law student. She has several years under her belt of hounding after research that focuses on menstruating humans, as well as coaching real life menstruating humans through their own ups and downs of hormone and health problems. Coach TL is a Functional Range Conditioning (i.e. mobility) Specialist---currently getting her MBA---with over two decades of experience intimately exploring the body, its limits, its movement patterns, and its capabilities with full-on fascination.

    While writing this book, both Coach Korra and TL have asked themselves what qualifies them to be the bearer of this information. The magnitude of the project loomed over them, but as they began to spread the word, teach, and create The Superpowers Planner, the obvious stories that lead them here began to surface.

Later you'll hear about Coach TL's shame around her menstruation, but SHAME in life was not prevalent for the outgoing dancer, academic bee, class president, safety patrol officer, and overall go-getter . . . as a matter a fact, the story that comes to mind on how she ended up here is from the 5th grade.

    The class was assigned reading groups, and the top readers of the class were the book leaders! TL was assigned "book leader" of the group that was to read non-fiction . . . all about the human body. This was much to her chagrin, since other groups were assigned "Pedro's Journey" and other stories---fiction was much more engaging than body parts. Long story short, the groups needed to present projects about their books to the class. And being the overachiever she was, she produced a full broadcast about the body. Since they were only 10 years old at the time, no one in the class wanted to be the anchor on the topic of "Private Parts", so TL did an entire 10-minute presentation on the vagina and it's canal up to the uterus and its purpose/function.

She did it with confidence and not breaking into a smile once. Presentation day came with a twist; it was also field trip day, meaning chaperones were in the room. Both of TL's parents were present.

When the presentation happened, no one in the room could stop giggling . . . including the red faces of the Steeles. No disrespect to Momma and Papa Steele (they have always been the most supportive cheerleaders), but TL couldn't figure out why it was so strange to chat about the vagina . . . which was a part of her body . . . but no one blinked an eye when we discussed noses. This anecdote is all to say, Coach TL has always been hyper curious, while also not seeing any sense in stigma. These qualities led her on this path, and she feels lucky to have Coach Korra to journey with.

Coach Korra has always been a writer and a reader. Even before she could sing the alphabet song, she was scribbling on legal pads "writing" out stories she could never actually read back (because again, it was literal scribble). And she can still remember the sensation of giddy joy when she read three whole American Girl Doll books in one night. At each finished book, she flew into her parents' room to proclaim her achievement. And, although her parents were probably less than thrilled the *third* time she burst into their bedroom that evening, the hunger to consume *more books* only grew stronger. Years later, her mom gave her a book published by the American Girl Doll company about female puberty, and it was the first book she shied away from---at first.

Coach Korra can still recall her confusion at the diagram of how to insert a tampon. *It goes WHERE?* But that book provided an important tonal difference from the talks of menstruation she experienced everywhere else. It seemed like the world was determined to only speak of periods in a hushed whisper---with commercials of women anxiously handing off tampons in hiding, or the downcast eyes of other teens after their pad or tampon wrapper crinkled from inside the school bathroom stall.

Meanwhile, the American Girl Doll book of puberty didn't bat an eye at things like illustrations of pubic hair, the notion of *fertility*, or even the sight of menstrual blood (the book showed it liberally). That book gave Coach Korra a completely different message about menstruation than the shame-filled one the world seemed to broadcast: that periods are *cool*. And now, with Coach TL's help, Coach Korra uses her love of both writing and reading to spread that same message
---only this time, when she writes things down, they can be read back with accuracy (for the most part).

Along this journey of body celebration, we will be laying out what we deem to be the *superpowers* of our menstrual cycle. This is the menstruating human's guide to biohacking & hormonal harmony---your crash course in a more productive and creative way of life that is built around your physiology. Because, unlike the mainstream's misbelief, it's not *just* about our periods.

This is our public service announcement about the misconceptions and longtime misunderstandings of the cyclical biology that about half of the population will experience; it is so much more than just menstruation. It is a cycle of power and it's bloody fantastic!

Chapter 1
Your Toolbox Tutorial

I'm sure if you took health class you have a basic understanding of your biology, but we believe that hearing it in updated language and a more encompassing understanding can be helpful. The average age of a person's 1st period is 12 years old, but this stage of life can occur anywhere between 8-17. Just as learning to walk and potty-train took time to learn and adjust to, so can your new menstruating body. Early on in our new body, our cycles can be unsettled or unsteady. Our human hardware is adjusting to a new gamut of hormones and very intense processes. The adjustment period can take years. All the while, we are learning to either support and celebrate our bodies' newfound superpowers, or we are listening to the hundreds of years of societal stigma; I hope we choose the former.

YOUR UTERUS
This mystical organ is where we can grow an

entirely new person! (Even if we choose not to---which is a completely valid choice---walking around with that possibility of power is pretty incredible.) In order to fully appreciate this power, we must feel it and get to know it. Your uterus is located between your hips, just above your pubic bone, and it's connected to the vagina via the cervix---which is the anchor for your reproductive system in the body.

Every cycle (timing varies per person) the uterus's blood cells mix with tissue to create a thick lining that is nest-like within the innermost layer, the endometrium. Once the signals have been made that there is no embryo ready for pregnancy, the uterus lets go and thus we shed that nest-like lining, aka our period. The muscles of your myometrium, the thick middle layer of the uterus, contract in order to remove all traces of a nest. (If you feel squeezed in all directions, never fear; you are!)

Meet your Uterus:

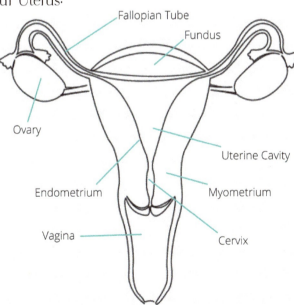

Note: no uterus looks exactly the same---just like most of what we discuss in this book, we are all different

and there is biodiversity amongst menstruating bodies when it comes to our reproductive system (i.e., varying vaginal lengths/shapes).

YOUR OVARIES

Because we focus on the absence or presence of blood so often, we accidently snub the real superstar of our cycle: OVULATION! Without it, hormones wouldn't even be present for us. We have pockets of pearls waiting behind the curtain of our pelvis, one on either side of the uterus, called oocytes.

The ovaries, our primary reproductive organs, are in constant communication with our pituitary gland (a small part of the brain). This conversation is what gives us our cycles, and how an egg is released every month.

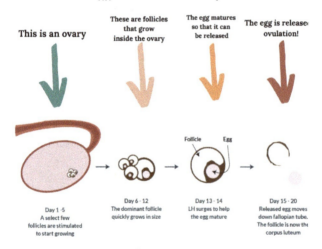

BIOLOGICALLY MALE & BIOLOGICALLY FEMALE

Humans are made of cells and tissues and matter---all of us---but one large differing factor in our biology is the menstrual cycle. The tissues that make up ovaries are used in utero to create testicles, which are important for male biology. Testicles produce testosterone, the star hormone in males. This is the driver of their cycle which runs its course in a 24-hour period.

Your Toolbox to Unleash Your Superpowers

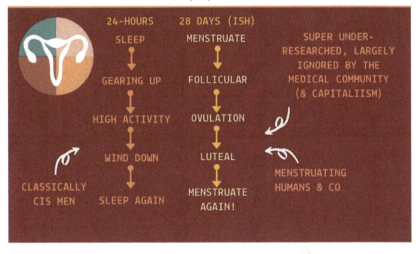

24-hour cycle = Circadian Rhythm
28(ish)-day cycle = Infradian Rhythm

    This Chart shows how the biological male cycle occurs. Testosterone is highest in the morning (as is sexual desire and focus); these drop as the day grinds onward. Collaboration is best in the afternoon, since the "I have shit to do, move out of the way" mentality wears off around then. Difficult communication is best left for the evening because levels are the lowest, before replenishment during the rem cycle. If you are biologically male you can wake up, walk out your door, and feel like the world is made for you---because it is.

    Daily activities, schedules, environments, and so much more are set up for male biology and the circadian cycle. When you walk into a building, the AC is set for your comfort, aka thermostats are set for an average temperature comfortable for men. Calendars for meetings and food are set up based on the circadian rhythm, and they are based on the assumption that we are the same every day. As if we rise and set like the sun. Biological females aren't even studied because we are considered hormonal anomalies. Our cycle is largely unknown globally, and we (male, female, non-binary, etc.) are being obliged to adhere to the biological male (circadian) cycle. No appreciation for deviation, we must be the SAME. Every. Day!

However, we as biological females don't just have one way of being that gradually dissipates over the course of the day and then renews with the sunrise. We are NOT ruled by the sun, but instead the moon! Our cycle, the Infradian Rhythm, is structured over the course of a month. Within each cycle there are two major hormonal events: ovulation and menstruation. While these events are only part of the month, we are always actively in them or preparing for them. We have four states of being that are cyclical each month: Menstruation, Follicular, Ovulation, and Luteal.

Because of the complexity and lack of knowledge around the infradian rhythm, society has deemed our hormones too complicated and, therefore, we get labeled TOO everything (emotional, irrational, unpredictable, etc.). This leaves a little over half the population in a constant state of adjusting to a normal that doesn't fit; it takes away the GO WITH THE FLOW mentality and makes us battle our way upstream. And although this conversation can be difficult, and some folks fear being reduced to their biology and its perceived limitations, it's vital we begin to live in a world that allows our brains and bodies to work within our cyclical nature.

Infradian Vs Circadian

Current productivity science is steeped in the 24-hour hormone cycle, the circadian rhythm:

Wake up
Work out
Do deep work
Network
Wind down
Sleep
Repeat

The infradian rhythm runs the same way, only the phases are stretched out from mere hours to days. And because we live in them longer we reap each phases gifts more deeply. I call them superpowers. But first, let's get familiar with what these phases are: the different phases of your cycle.

Your Toolbox to Unleash Your Superpowers

*Although AFAB (assigned female at birth) bodies do have a circadian cycle, our menstruating bodies don't adhere to that biological clock. We run on the infradian cycle until perimenopause, when we begin, once again, to run on the 24-hour cycle.

Next up . . . the infradian cycle close up:

- Hopefully, all the hormones have cleared out and you're running on just a little bit of testosterone.
- The first 2 days of your period, your period powers are most potent. Focus on review, rest, and relying on intuition.
- PMS symptoms set in, telling you what your past cycle needed. Slow down to listen to your body's wants.
- On day 3 you get an estrogen kick to prep for ovulation and you straddle both period and follicular. Take what you learned in reviewing to improve and plan.
- This ample cortisol supply means working too hard can burn you out easier. Completing tasks and making space for luxuriating and rest can ease the cortisol levels and make for a healthier progesterone bump.
- As estrogen rises, so does your energy. Your brain is best at taking in new information and thinking creatively.
- Your body breaks down estrogen and builds up progesterone only to break it down again. Your body is more apt to produce cortisol now, a stress hormone.
- A follicle in your ovary prepares an egg for ovulation.
- The first few days of luteal are like ovulatory. Ride that estrogen wave!
- An egg is released from your ovary and travels down the fallopian tube, waiting to be fertilized or to disintegrate. You are only actually fertile for one day but you will feel this zone for almost a full week.
- Estrogen peaks, as does your 'power.' Physical, mental, emotional - you name it. Socialize and collaborate, and ask the world for the impossible, you're more likely to get it.

Menstruation
2-8 days - Your period!

Luteal
11-20 days

pure Follicular
3-8 days

Ovulation
1 day

Flow Key

> **Note**
> The medical community deems day 1 to ovulation your Follicular Phase, and from after ovulation to your period the Luteal Phase, with your period and ovulation being "events" on top of this two phase cycle. We will still use that metric, only, for exponential purposes, we've separated pure Follicular from the rest, and sectioned out Luteal into sub-parts here.

* Don't know how to track your phases? Check out the abundance of cycle tracking apps. Ones that use a basal thermometer are going to give you - to the day - accuracy.

THE TWO HALVES OF YOUR CYCLE

Our cycles are broken into two halves: the follicular and luteal phases (which we are going to go more in-depth on in chapters 3 and 5). You can see in the circular chart on the previous page where our two big events (menstruation and ovulation) land within those phases, and how our month flows. Basically, the follicular phase is a build up toward the peak, and Luteal is the slide down. Have you heard the phrase, "What goes up, must come down"? When I (Coach TL) was told this in relation to my own body, I was offended. I pride myself on being an optimist, and the idea of not always having sunshine and roses was beyond me. When I sat with this ebb and flow for longer, I began to understand.

Each month there is a time to be, do, give, and take.

Carry these energy ebbs and flows with you as you journey through this book and learn about the brilliance that is your own human hardware.

TL;DR (TOO LONG; DIDN'T READ)
YOUR TOOLBOX TUTORIAL

» Your uterus and ovaries are your reproductive system that is in communication with the pituitary gland (brain)
» We all have a Circadian rhythm; but menstruating humans ALSO have the Infradian rhythm
» The world is set up for cis-male biology
» We have 4 parts to our Infradian Rhythm:
~Menstruation (the event)
~Follicular Phase (pure)
~Ovulation (the event)
~Luteal Phase
» Our bodies are incredible and have so many superpowers packed into our month that we have a time to:
~Be
~Do
~Give
~Take

Chapter 2
Menstruation (The Event)

The event of menstruation, aka our periods, is typically considered to be the big downer of our biology. From the cramps to the mood swings to the fatigue to the literal bloody mess, this part of our biology has been used to shame menstruating bodies into a smaller, tighter mold for centuries. This is why our talk about superpowers is going to start with the stereotyped "worst" part of our cycles, our period.

Let's first talk about what our periods even are. The first day of our periods are now seen as the first day of our follicular phase (which has three parts to it: our bleeds, the pure follicular phase, and then the event of ovulation---but we'll dig deeper into that later.) So yes, you're reading that right, menstruating is no longer considered to be an actual phase of the menstrual cycle. We know, it's a little backwards. The entire cycle is renowned for the bleeding part, and yet the medical community has determined that it's not a phase of our hormonal cycle at all, but rather a part of our uterine cycle. And it is for this reason that we're going to refer to our periods as events in this book, likewise with ovulation.

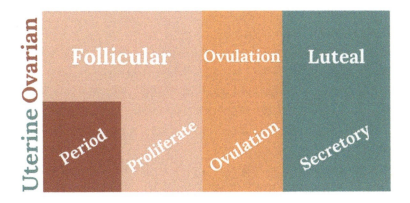

During our periods our uterus sheds its lining, which is the red stuff you see in the toilet bowl. It's not exactly blood (we can't use it to save someone dying of blood loss), but it does have a lot of blood cells in it. The lining of our uterus was made in the phase before to save us from a potential embryo. Why do we need to be protected from an embryo? Because embryos are hungry. Without the lush lining of our uterus re-growing every month, any embryo we created would be able to dig into the actual structure of our uterus and drain us of a significant amount of energy and nutrients. We need that lush lining of blood and nutrients to keep our own human hardware safe.

A study was done on mice where embryos were "implanted" in different tissues of the mouse's body, and each time the embryo wreaked absolute havoc and destroyed the poor mouse. But when implanted in a fully prepared mouse uterus, the mouse was able to maintain a pregnancy and keep its own life. Some scientists theorize that the lining of the uterus isn't designed to helpfully nurture and coddle a hungry embryo, but instead creates a hospitable environment for the embryo that puts enough breaks on the embryo's appetite to allow the surrounding body to survive. It turns out, lush uterine linings are how mammals can slowly build an entirely new organism without losing their lives.

So, yeah, we think it's pretty rad.

As for the shedding of the uterine lining, that seems to be mainly limited to primates. Most mammals don't bleed between ovulations; instead, their body reabsorbs the lining as a part of their reproductive cycle. So the process of *shedding* the lining is almost exclusively a primate thing.

We've been fascinated by what made that difference come about, and the answer seems to lie in the complexity of primate pregnancies. Primates tend to only have one baby at a time, and our brains are so energy-demanding that each offspring takes a *lot* of energy from the parent to develop. Therefore, primates can't afford mistakes; every baby we make has to meet rigorous biological standards to ensure that it's as healthy and as apt for survival as possible. The best theory we've come across is that we developed this process as a way to save our bodies from *non-viable* pregnancies.

See, when an embryo is made and implants itself into the uterine lining, it sends out a warning signal to our bodies; a little "Hey! I'm here! Start the process of pregnancy!" message. And for that embryo to not tell our bodies that it's here and ready to start demanding resources is a big red flag that this embryo isn't up to code. Especially if this was happening way back when we were still evolving and fire was a foreign concept, let alone medical intervention. Back then, an uncooperative pregnancy would have killed us. So our bodies evolved a safety net,* the monthly flushing of the uterine lining, to be sure that viable embryos were allowed to stay.

Our bodies also developed this process as a way to flush out healthy embryos that our hardware isn't equipped to provide for. For example, the COVID-19 vaccine has been jump-starting periods in menstruating humans ("COVID-19..." 2022). This phenomenon has been coined "the red wave" and it most likely happens because our bodies are using an already made process to protect ourselves from having to undergo two extremely energy-intensive processes at once. To put it simply, our human hardware has figured out, through several millennia of evolution, that if it has to choose between entering cooperation with a new embryo or fending off a perceived deadly virus, it would rather fight the virus. Fighting the virus will keep us alive, agreeing to take on the process of baby-making will not. So, our bodies induce a period to "flush out" any potential embryos we might have made recently so our energy and resources can get channeled into reacting to the vaccine.

So far, this is the best theory we've come across as for *why* we developed the process of shedding our uterine lining. And it's rather heart-warming. Our bodies bleed once a cycle as a way to be absolutely sure that they can continue to take care of us as best as possible. Turns out our periods are looking out for us! So let's mend our relationship with them and celebrate their support, benefits, and power!

Note: not every pregnancy is biologically healthy. We evolved this one trait to help each offspring be as healthy as possible---but it's not a foolproof system.

REPORT CARD

Have you ever heard that friendship song? 'A circle is round and has no end?' That's what our infradian rhythm is like, and our periods are the prime example of that because while they kick off the start of our follicular phase, they also act as *report cards* for our month-ish prior. An ending and a beginning all at once. In fact, that *report card* aspect of our periods is the first superpower we're going to talk about--- let's do it!

OK, *report card*. The symptoms, thoughts, and feelings that come up for us when the menstruation event begins are data points that tell us how well we did or didn't support ourselves and our needs in the month-ish before. And we mean that *everything* is a data point.

» *Cramps*
» *Fatigue*
» *Acne*
» *Heightened emotions*
» *Brain fog*
» *Appetite changes/Nausea*
» *Bloating*
» *Tender breasts*
» *Headaches*
» *Backaches*
» *Cravings*
» *Insomnia*
» *Changes in bowel movements*
» *Low energy*
» *Strong internal compass*
» *Needing alone time*

It's all data. But data by itself is useless unless we can draw conclusions from it. So how do we interpret this data? Well the answer to that is going to be different for everyone. To learn to interpret your own data points, we recommend keeping a journal (or checking out The Superpowers Planner) to stay on top of what goes into and what comes out of your cycle. Let's run through a hypothetical to show you what we mean.

Let's say we get our period and we are massively fatigued. During our luteal phase, did we run ourselves ragged, or did we maybe not eat enough to support our heightened luteal metabolism? It's never a coincidence, and in this common hypothetical, the cause and effect sync up. Fatigue is our body's way of saying that we are depleted and we need more sources of energy (i.e., sleep and food). Solution? Eat more, sleep more, and definitely eat and sleep more in the next luteal phase.

Let's look at another: are we in massive pain from period cramps? Period cramps can have a lot of causes, but the biggest cause is pelvic tension, which we can get from lack of movement, too much movement, or poor nutrition. So let's look back; throughout our month(ish) did we barely move our bodies throughout the day---or did we push through our workouts too much? Did we give too little attention to activities that would relax our overworked bodies, especially during the parts of our month-ish when we needed it most? Or maybe we moved as much as we needed to but ate bland, nutrient-poor food, and our pelvic muscles are taking the opportunity to ring the bell for the sake of our whole body.

There is no universal cheat sheet for all of the period symptoms out there because, as we discussed, we are all so different. But by exploring how removing or adding resources during your cycle affects your next period, we can create our own cheat sheet.

Coach Korra, for example, knows that eating canola/rapeseed oil outside of her pure follicular phase makes her breasts sore and increases her cramps, and that cutting carbs in her luteal phase makes for a bloated, exhausted, and emotional bleeding time. So she uses olive oil and grass-fed butter for most of her month and indulges every craving she has in her luteal phase with carb-dense foods.

Meanwhile Coach TL knows that when she gives into lethargy in her luteal phase and is mainly inactive, her bleeding event is painful and laborious. Therefore, she maintains an active lifestyle throughout the entirety of her cycle, tweaking the input effort and impact during each part of her month-ish.

Some experts, like researcher and practitioner Alisa Vitti of FLO Living, even say that this report card lens can manifest through the actual color of our bleeds---although official Western medicine has yet to test this out, so go forth from here with a grain of salt.

Purple bleeds can mean that you have a slight estrogen dominance. This means you didn't break down *enough* estrogen during your luteal phase, and, if not rebalanced, can mean that you're always operating with just a little too much estrogen for where your body is comfortable. This can be forewarned during your cycle with acne, brain fog, and/or fatigue during your ovulation event when estrogen is peaking. And can be rebalanced by supporting your liver all cycle long and by supporting your luteal phase (see further resources in Chapter 5). Purple bleeds are also associated with polycystic ovary syndrome (PCOS)* and normally come as a thick flow with plenty of blood clots.

Brown bleeds can mean that you're not building up enough progesterone during your luteal phase which can be caused from a myriad of factors such as too much stress during the luteal phase, too little complex carbs, too many sugary foods and drinks, or too little sleep---to name a few. Too low progesterone can be felt in the luteal phase with consistent burn out, nightmares and night sweats, consistent low energy, low moods, and mood swings. We know that the traits progesterone brings to the table aren't fun, but during our luteal phase, if our bodies don't have enough of it, the side effects can be even worse than if progesterone never showed up at all. And we'll talk even more about this in Chapter 5.

Pink bleeds can mean that you're not producing enough estrogen and is normally forewarned by elongated cycles, inconsistent cycles, and really late ovulations (if ovulation happens at all). Because low estrogen affects ovulation so severely, issues with this imbalance can lead to a slump during an innately super-charged time. Thankfully, like all of the other imbalances, all a pink bleed may be asking for is support during your cycle. In Coach Korra's practice, she's found the biggest factor in shifting a pink bleed is to engage with sugar less consistently with a method called "crowding out" that we'll explain later in Chapter 5.

And lastly, *red* bleeds can mean that between estrogen and progesterone, your hormones are pretty balanced.

When we view our periods this way---as a monthly check-in with how our bodies are doing---our periods can become less of a burden and more of an inbox. What messages did our bodies tell us during our cycle? What are they saying, and how can we respond during our next cycle to give them the support they need?

Now, this paradigm applies not only to our physical symptoms, but to our emotional ones as well. And this is so fascinating that we've made it a second superpower.

*For folks with premenstrual dysphoric disorder (PMDD), endometriosis, and PCOS, this rule of thumb still holds true, however most of the data points will be tying back to the imbalances that are tipping your cycle into something to pathologize. We will dive into these conditions in chapter 11.

INTUITION

On top of the report card feature of our periods, there is something else that makes this event so *powerful*. During our menstrual event (the first two days especially) the two halves of our brain talk to each other more than any other brain on any other hormone bath. This gives us the superpower of *intuition*. Now, everyone has intuition, but brains that are actively menstruating take that "normal" level of intuition to superhuman heights.

Normally, we go about the world taking in data. Our conscious minds are aware of some stuff (the light turned green, he's talking to me, those flowers really brighten up the room), and our *subconscious* minds are aware of so much *more*. It works like an iceberg. The perceptions that you're aware of are above the water, but below the water the iceberg is, at minimum, twice as large. And our processing systems work similarly.

What intuition does is take all of the data our subconscious mind has perceived (or is perceiving) and draws a deeper conclusion. Have you ever been walking home alone at night and come across different sets of lone strangers? You might have noticed that one sent your adrenaline racing, had you reaching for your phone or something for protection, and that the other person just made you wary in general. That was your intuition picking up signals from the potentially dangerous person, tying them into lessons you've already learned, and sounding the alarm that *they are dangerous*.

Intuition is also that extra sense that tells us when someone is staring at us and the loudest subconscious voice that helps us decide between options when we think we're just guessing. It also comes into play when we're interacting with animals or people who don't speak the same language as us. It can be the quiet whisper that plants the seeds of ideas in the conscious mind, or the brilliant lightbulb that

suddenly makes everything feel clear. Dial into your intuition and ponder big questions like:
- » How do I feel about the month I just had?
- » What will I grow and give to life next?

Brains that are on their periods, that are actively menstruating, have this lightbulb-form of intuition in spades. But why don't we praise this time, then? Why is the stereotype of periods that we become overly emotional, with short tempers and a tenuous grasp on logic?

Let's be clear, intuition *is* logical, but sometimes it doesn't show all of the work. Instead of going from A to B to C to D, which is what happens in our conscious minds, intuition takes in the trigger of A and tells you to jump to your conclusion of D. The steps in the middle all get left behind in our subconscious perceptions. Our brain is still working, it's just working at hyper speed. So we think we've gone looney, coming up with conclusions that don't have a clear, consciously thought out path or stimulus. But even though we *feel* crazy, we're not. And to make matters even more complicated, our intuition isn't the only thing that makes us feel crazy. Let's talk about mood swings.

The mood swings you might experience on your periods can come from a myriad of factors, and none of them are worthy of being shamed.

One factor is that hormonal imbalances, like the ones we touched on with the physical report card superpower of our periods, can give our emotional brain chemistry a run for its money (not breaking down enough estrogen before our period, or having too low a progesterone bump in the luteal phase for examples).

If this is where you fit, those mood swings are messages from your body to take care of your hormonal health. And for that, we recommend first cataloguing your symptoms and following the leads to the triggers that started them. But we want to impress that these mood swings are not our body's goal during our menstrual events, just an inconvenience/side effect of a greater issue/etc.

Two, a lot of us do not have the support or space to feel our feelings all month. For example, instead of dealing with the feelings of resentment and hurt when our partner leaves us with all of the housework, we may get hit with some very deep and (seemingly over-proportional) anger and anxiety towards them. But this isn't a sign that you, deep down, hate your partner. Rather, it's the true depth of your pain at being left to play housekeeper when you've asked them *repeatedly to empty out the whole dishwasher.*

When we engage with emotional self-care all month, and demand the space to validate how we feel, we can help ourselves turn a moody period into an invaluable tool for self-growth. The key here is to get a support system in place. Get a therapist, and communicate your needs to your partner---ask for help! The days of the esteemed martyr are over; long live the generous communicator and self-accepter! Because the truth is that it's not an over-emotional response, it is the accumulation of how we've been feeling all month.

The third factor, and the last we'll mention (although there are undoubtedly more), is that we live in a toxic patriarchy! (If you didn't know, surprise!) Not all patriarchies are toxic, but ours is, and it has always needed to step on anyone who isn't a cis-white-hetero man.

Prior to current cultural norms, anthropologists theorized that our earliest cultural practices including politics, art, and religion were organized around menstruation. WHAT?! In the book, *Blood Relations* by Chris Knight (1995), he explains how, essentially, it was the females who likely created the taboo---not because it was shameful, but because it was a time to establish their bodies as sacred. Long story short (go read the book if you want more gritty details)---the females went on sex strikes during their time of month in order to ensure their children were fed . . . it was their way of demanding help and setting boundaries. While the women gathered to bleed, the men went out to hunt. No meat = no sex. It became a ritual that initially empowered the menstruators, but eventually backfired (most likely during the ice age). When the planet began to change, hunting practices did too. Therefore, women lost their power in ritual and the spaces that were once honored as safe for bleeding became the spaces for men to gather and exclude the menstruators . . . starting what is now our prevalent patriarchal principles.

Since our periods are the time when all of our subconscious perceptions become solidified and amplified, our periods became the red flag to the patriarchal system. In a way, this superpower of our periods is kind of like the *gaslighting-extinguisher*, reminding us of our true feelings in spite of what the external world might be telling us. So go forth, intuitive one, and *listen to yourself!*

For folks with PMDD, clinical depression, borderline personality disorder (BPD), or other hormonal/mental disorders, this superpower might turn completely on its head and go from gift to curse. So let us make this very clear: Intuition never comes from a place of fear or anxiety and it will never tell you to take your own life. If you dread your bleeding days because of some righteously egregious upheaval of your sense of self-preservation and sense of reality, please, please, please talk to your gyno and therapist about it so you can get the help you need to support whatever chemical or hormonal imbalance that is harming you. Our periods did not evolve to be a monthly time of self-torture.

"Ok," You may be thinking. "So my period is actually not so bad. But how long does this last? Because I know tons of folks who have really long or really light periods. If I barely need a panty-liner, am I still super intuitive?" And, even if you weren't thinking that, it's a great question. So we're going to take the time to answer it.

All of our period superpowers are most potent on days one and two of our bleeds. (And for folks who get some pre-period spotting, we're talking about the first day of your bleed that makes you shove aside your nicer underwear for a later day.) On day three of our periods, we get a little kick of estrogen to start off our ensuing climb to ovulation. And when that influx of estrogen comes, we are straddling period powers and follicular powers. In short, the few days before our periods and the latter days of our bleeds are still graced with our period's superpowers, but the first and second day of undeniable period flow are the most potent for period superpowers.

The one period superpower that holds its potency beyond the first two days of our bleed is really a physical superpower, one most might not associate with their periods: strength.

WE'RE STRONG AF

If you flip back to the graph of our cycle on page 20 showing the example of balanced hormones, the days straddling the start of our periods are when the hormone testosterone is the most potent of the big three hormones we've been talking about. And remember, it doesn't mean that we're making *more* testosterone, just that there isn't much progesterone or estrogen to talk over it. But still, testosterone is a really driven performance enhancer.

For folks who exercise, this means that each of our periods can affect our workouts in one of two ways.

One way is the stereotype of a body actively bleeding: tired and struggling through physical challenges that, on any other day, would be a breeze. This can be due to the fact that when we're bleeding our bodies are, y'know, *bleeding*---actively *shedding the lining of an organ*. It's pretty badass but it's also a lot of work. And for some bodies, the act of shedding that lining is a workout all on its own. As Coach Korra has said, "You think you're being lazy, watching

TV with a bag of chips, but internally your body is at the gym."

But this can also be due to hormonal imbalances (meaning testosterone *isn't* the most potent hormone that day), or from not taking care of our human hardware---although honestly the two usually go hand in hand. With either cause, the best way to take control of a fatigued period is to accept that a slowed pace and extra recoup time are exactly what your body needs.

The second way is the total opposite, an *energized* period. Fully balanced hormones and a body that's received the crucial support it needs can give us the ability to barely flinch at the prospect of *shedding the lining of an inner organ*. It's a winning combination to allow that testosterone potency that we talked about to shine! In fewer words: we have the potential to be *really* dang *strong* during our menstrual events. And this superpower can stretch out beyond just days one and two of our bleeds, too.

If you are a few days away from your period, and you feel solid and physically grounded in your human hardware, hit the gym or the mat or the bike and *go for your max*. Folks who consistently experience periods like this may even want to schedule competitions while they're bleeding!

And if you're sitting there shaking your head because it sounds so far-fetched, let us introduce you to Paula Radcliffe. She broke world records while running through period cramps! She's also spoken up about many fellow runners who fail their races because they succumbed to uninformed pressure to control when their periods come by taking medications. She even has called out for more studies to be done on sports performance in relation to the menstrual cycle to give menstruating athletes the proper chance they deserve.

Paula Radcliffe said it best when she noted, "Too often in sport, doctors are men and they don't understand" ("Paula Radcliffe...", 2015).

Talk about breaking period stigmas, right?

With benefits like these, we can exhale and appreciate our cycle, rather than worry about that one event that gets stereotyped as "bad." In reality, our hormone levels at that moment can be a booster to achieving great things. Remember when we discussed the theory that we evolved to have periods to expunge any potential, uncooperative pregnancy? Well, by the time you're actively bleeding, your human hardware has rid itself of an unnecessary responsibility. Therefore, it gets to enter a more relaxed state, clearing the way for possibility and allowing your personal power to focus on exertion. It's why our last big period superpower is strength.

Hey, did you know that your body is *incredible*? Because it is.

BLEEDING (SIDEKICK OF A SUPERPOWER)

Let's focus for a moment on the idea that *menstruating humans are the only humans who can walk around, actively bleeding, and not even need so much as a Band-Aid.* We wake up in pools of our own blood, *shrug*, and put in a tampon "just to keep things neater." How many times have we tried to hide the fact that our bodies are secretly shedding the entire lining of an organ? What's that phrase? *Anything you can do, I can do bleeding.*

Superhuman! We say. Warrior! We cheer. *Talk about a badass!* But there are some histories, cultures, and religions that deem menstruating humans as "lesser" because our bleeds are seen as intrinsically "dirty." Well, that's plain hogwash, we say. Not only is our period blood an indicator of how *badass* we are, but it's also actually a kind of sidekick type of superpower!

PLANTS LOVE IT

Period blood is so nutrient rich, it can literally take infertile soil and make it fertile (more or less). Yeah. Our periods are amazing natural fertilizers---and we mean *amazing*. Coach Korra, ever the self-experimenter, found out about this mini super power, and had to test it out for herself. She poured a solution of her menstrual cup contents and water over a *dead, dead* patch of grainy dirt by her home at the time. She only poured it once, but a few days later the once *dead, dead* patch of dirt was *thriving* with new plant growth. And that's just one account of many of plants thriving off of period blood.

Along with being potentially inhospitable for embryos, the lining of our uterus is also nutrient rich to keep that embryo satiated enough that it doesn't eat *us*. And when we shed that lining, all of the nutrients go with it. Plants *love* those nutrients. But before you go dumping your menstrual cup over your potted African violets, understand that our period blood is an *intense* fertilizer. Maybe it's a part of what protects us from the appetite of a hungry embryo, but adding too much period blood to plants can actually burn them. Most at risk is the plant's root system, which can be disintegrated by period blood's pH. A good rule of thumb is one teaspoon/tablespoon of period blood (half of a whole menstrual cup's worth) per *quart* of water, at least.

There are some experts who warn that adding period blood to soil can be harmful because of the microbes contained in our period blood. (Microbes are good and bad bacteria, fungi, viruses, and archaea---we'll talk more about microbes soon, don't worry!). Soil has its own microbiome that needs to be kept healthy and happy, but diluting period blood is a good way to curtail any microbe issues that could arise---and it saves the soil's pH as well!

Ever since that one experiment years ago, Coach Korra has been fertilizing her plants and gardens with her menstrual cup and she's only had beautifully positive experiences. In her words, "Once a month everyone gets some period blood and water solution, and around the same time every month, everyone starts sprouting out new leaves!" But just as all gardens are different, so are people's bleeds, so we advise using this sidekick of a superpower with curiosity instead of reckless abandon.

    Some people get really freaked out by this superpower, and we understand---using period blood as a fertilizer is not for everyone. But we have to include it because our bleeds carry *so much stigma* from across different cultures and religions; a common word used to describe them is "dirty." However, when we utilize our bleeds with intention and care, our period blood can be a magnificent resource for fertility and growth. We can literally *nourish soil* in a way that no one else can, without even needing an emergency kit on hand. And we do it naturally, without needing to injure ourselves or perform a blood sacrifice like some cultures used to for good harvest. Again, we have to say: *talk about badass!*

    *For anyone wondering if we can fix our world's dead swaths of farm land with period blood, we recommend checking out the book or Netflix documentary, Kiss the Ground, *because our agricultural issues are more complex than a simple lack of nutrients.*

USING THESE SUPERPOWERS

    If your head is spinning, take this as an opportunity to breathe. We covered a lot of ground---and that ground is saturated by a history of oppression, shame, and pain (which is discussed in Chapter 9)---so it makes sense if you need to take a moment to rethink and process some things.

    And for our folks with PMDD, Endometriosis, and PCOS, we have a whole chapter for you and your cycle, *plus* further resources so that you can come to love your period, too. Like we said before, we're done turning people into asterisks here. *Every* menstruating human deserves to love their body as much as their body loves them.

    Your period is not bad.

    Your period is an amazing part of your menstrual biology.

    Your human hardware is downright <u>glorious</u>.

    Now that we've covered what superpowers our periods endow us with, let's dig into *how* to use these powers so they're not just abstract ideas. When you distill the period superpowers down into a type of *energy*, you get the superpower of *review* (time to BE). Our periods are the best time to *reassess*, *reflect*, and *reprocess*; all to come to new conclusions. And, as we will keep saying, this doesn't mean that you cannot review things outside of your menstrual event, just that reviewing during your menstrual event will be far more *productive* and *helpful* than reviewing at other times of our cycle.

    This means that if you are a student, your menstrual event is an opportune time to reread your class notes and organize your understanding of difficult concepts in your education.

    If you're someone who writes a lot for a living or for education, your period is an invaluable time to edit what you've written and finalize your work before handing it in or publishing it.

    If you work in a management position, your period is the most helpful time to go over performance reviews.

    If you are a creative type, your period is the most opportune time to reflect on your current projects and how they are coming along.

    If you live in the *go-go-go* of the American capitalist society, you might not know where to start with this whole reflection thing. For that reason, we're including some reflection questions to get you started. Back in May of 2021, we released The Superpowers Planner, a productivity planner for menstruating humans to achieve their peak performance, no matter their goals. And at the end of each month, during the period week, we included some of these reflection questions---because despite what the "work hard, play hard" paradigm suggests, rest and reflection are a *necessary* part of every cycle. Just ask mother nature!

Lastly, if you are someone who engages with exercise (or as Coach TL calls anything that gets your body moving in a nourishing way, wiggles) and you feel like your period is well-nourished, then this is a great time to *go for gold.* Whatever your favorite form of wiggling is, aim to set your personal record while you're bleeding like a badass warrior!

» *How do I feel about my last month/cycle?*
» *What can I celebrate this month/cycle?*
» *What were my biggest lessons?*
» *How can I transmute this reflection into planning?*
» *What habits do I want to release and start?*

TL;DR MENSTRUATION
(THE EVENT)

- *Our menstruation phase is full of BE-ing energy*
- *The act of bleeding once a cycle serves a purpose to potentially save us from uncooperative pregnancies ---> It's one of the many ways our human hardware takes care of us!*
- *Our periods' superpowers are:*
    - *~Acting as a report card for our hormonal month(ish)*
    - *~Intuition*
    - *~Super strength*
- *Our bleeds are an amazing fertilizer!*
- *Reflection is a necessary part of every cycle and process.*
- *This is a time when we can kick our workouts into high gear (even break world records)!*

Chapter 3
Follicular Phase (Pure)

As mentioned earlier, the follicular phase spans the whole range of time from the first day of our periods through to ovulation. The new consensus in the medical community is that there are two hormonal phases to our cycle: the follicular and luteal phases. This chapter is going to talk about the first one!

The follicular phase encapsulates the two big *events* of the infradian rhythm, *menstruation* and *ovulation*---even though those two events couldn't feel more different experientially. And while we are keeping as close to the medically correct science as possible, we are writing this book for people who *live* the infradian rhythm. So, for the purposes of this book, when we talk about the follicular phase, we are talking about the part of the follicular phase that doesn't overlap with our periods or ovulation---unless otherwise noted.

UNLEASH YOUR SUPERPOWERS

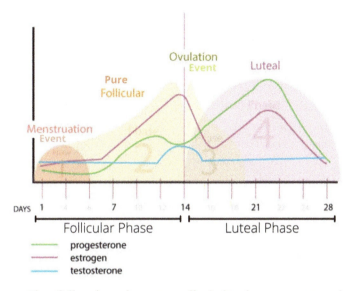

The follicular phase is called this because it's when our bodies prepare a *follicle* to be readied into an egg and released.

As beings born with ovaries, we are born with all of the eggs (sex cells, gametes) that we will ever need. But they're not all perfectly cooked eggs---ready and raring to go. They're in a pre-cooked state, so to speak, as follicles. Each follicle gets its own cluster of nurse cells to look after it while inside the ovary. They also prepare it to be a fully realized egg should it ever be selected as the egg to "drop" in one of our many cycles as a menstruating human.

While our ovary is preparing an egg during the follicular phase, estrogen is rising. As we mentioned in the previous chapter, we get a little kick of estrogen on day three of our periods and that little kick keeps climbing until it peaks at ovulation. Once our periods end (when we feel you can safely wear white underwear or go swimming without wearing period products), we've already gained enough estrogen to begin to feel the superpowers of the pure follicular phase.

This is when we feel the power of estrogen gaining momentum. In this time, we are ready to attack a problem head on, absorb new information, and perform in creative ways. We become solution-oriented, and we can feel like we are winning at life---because this is a time in our cyclical journey where we are suited to tackle what is acclaimed in the bro-hustle (i.e., linear) life.

The superpowers of the follicular phase are *exciting*. If you follow even the basics of Eastern medicine, you can think of the pure follicular phase and ovulation event as a *yang* time. Our bodies and brains are *raring* to go. They want to be active, to *do, achieve, seek,* and *start* things.

This gives us a leg up compared to our circadian-only friends and family, because while they only experience some of this *do* energy for a few hours every day---we have it for *multiple* days. And this brand of energetics, this *DO* energy, leads us to our first superpower.

STRESS? WHAT STRESS?

During the follicular phase, life's stressors are, well, less stressful! All of this *do*-ing energy can take on multiple projects and tasks at once like it's a breeze! And there are a few components of the follicular phase that give us this superpower. Let's start with the hormonal variety: low progesterone.

During the follicular phase we make very low levels of the hormone progesterone. Progesterone, if you remember, is considered a sex hormone, but is also a precursor to the stress hormone, cortisol. Producing low levels of progesterone means that our bodies will make less cortisol in reaction to a stressful stimulus. So, when a stressful event happens (you missed your alarm, you got handed three days of work to finish in an hour, you literally spilled milk), our bodies don't feel overwhelmed by the stress.

Don't worry, you'll still understand that the situation is stressful. And that's a good thing, by the way. Our bodies' stress systems are what allowed us to survive in the wild without claws and fangs, long before we figured out how to make tools. But in this phase, we're less likely to be *consumed* by our stress. As Jinkx Monsoon of RuPaul's drag race used to say, "water off a duck's back." We perceive the stress, but it doesn't affect us as deeply. And the ability to roll with the punches from having low progesterone becomes even more supercharged when we talk about a really *joyful* effect of the follicular phase's increasing estrogen levels.

MOOD & RESILIENCY

This might not sound like the superpower of a comic book character, but our moods affect *everything* in our bodies---from stress levels to sleep to food cravings to energy levels and even to some forms of chronic pain! We can actually store our emotions in our human hardware when we don't process them. (Example: we store trauma and stress emotions in our iliopsoas---which is a large contributor to why folks feel ticklish or tight in their hip flexors.) Plus, our brains can't tell the difference between emotional pain and physical pain (Fogel 2012)---so, ah, yeah! Our moods are pretty important!

And in our follicular phase our moods are primed to keep getting better and better, and here's why: the hormone that is climbing all throughout the entire follicular phase, estrogen, helps dopamine, a happy hormone, bind to receptors easier. In fact, there is even some research that suggests estrogen increases the *number* of receptors for which dopamine can bind.

How cool is that! This means that during the entire follicular phase (in this case, from day three of our periods to ovulation) we have a biologically equipped weapon to keep the clouds at bay---and even to cut through brain fog! *Estrogen!*

This extra bonus of mood takes the follicular phase's decreased stress response and makes for the superpower of *resiliency.* In this life, bad things happen all of the time, but in the follicular phase we have multiple components making our bodies and brains super-juiced to handle the hardest stuff.

Plus, with the extra dopamine, we just plum-drum *feel good* during this phase.

Bonus Features:
Tip for our menstruating humans with attention deficit hyperactivity disorder (ADHD) or attention deficit disorder (ADD), depression, and other dopamine-affected mental states/illnesses: this can mean that you might feel fewer symptoms during your follicular phase and ovulation when estrogen is giving you a wink from behind the scenes. Alternatively, you might feel your symptoms more *during your luteal phase and early on in your period.*

For folks on medications, you may find it helpful to talk to your doctor about changing your dosages during your cycle, and for folks not on medications or who are self-medicating, taking your cycle into account can make a world of difference in managing your mental states'/illnesses' symptoms and attributes.

HEIGHTENED CREATIVITY, PLANNING, AND PROBLEM-SOLVING

With this decreased stress response and heightened mood, the follicular phase is primed for a third superpower, *superhuman creativity, planning, and problem-solving skills.* These may all sound like different skills, but in the pure follicular phase each of these superpowers is formed from the same stimuli: the extra dopamine, rising estrogen, and lessened stress response. And we use each of these

superpowers interchangeably depending on where within a process we find ourselves.
1. Problem-solving requires dexterous creativity and planning.
2. Creativity requires expressive problem-solving and agile planning.
3. Well-thought-out planning requires foreseen problem-solving and creativity.

They're all connected!

Now that we've established that these superpowers are connected, let's start our discussion of them with just one: planning. The pure follicular phase is set up to be the time when we're able to take everything good and bad that we reviewed and processed during our periods, and use them with a fresh mindset. We're able to process and come to emotional and clarifying conclusions during our periods, and then, in the beginning of our follicular phases, those emotional conclusions can be transmuted into actionable plans. *Do*-ing energy and superpowered planning at its finest!

In this phase we're also less likely to feel stonewalled by a problem, as our brains are primped and primed for thinking flexibly and finding new solutions to things---cue creativity and problem-solving! This is the best time to throw a bunch of ideas against the wall and see what sticks. With all of that dopamine and the lessened stress response, high stakes can automatically feel like pure motivation. We aren't as overwhelmed by the fear of what can go wrong and we can jump into the creative process of *"How many ways can this go right?"* It's when our imaginations have the energy and abundance to run boundless through the possibilities until we find a solution that works.

Let's go back to one of our examples from the stress superpower.

Say we needed to be up at 6:00 a.m. for an 8:30 presentation---but we were up so late with our brains buzzing about all of the new ways to approach points in our presentation that we didn't hit the hay until 1:00 a.m. Luckily, we don't need *as* much sleep in our follicular phase (our hormones here give us an energy boost, remember?). So we might miss our alarm and wake up at 7:15 a.m. We still don't have nearly enough time to have that calm and spacious morning we were counting on, but being in the follicular phase means our bodies can absorb the shock of the moment more easily. Then, we can quickly jump to the next part in a crisis: solving the problem.

    We bolt from the bed and decide, quickly, to throw on yesterday's outfit (the people at the meeting don't know we wore it yesterday, and picking out a new outfit would take too much time!). In the kitchen, our crisis-mode brains realize that the coffee machine takes 5 minutes to get a full cup going. We put our to-go mug at the ready and turn it on so we can gather our work materials while the water boils. Quickly brush the teeth, pull the hair back, and by the time we're ready to jump out the door, the coffee's ready.

    We skip morning rush hours because we put on our shoes after we arrive---we don't need shoes to operate a gas pedal---and magically we're *early* for the meeting (giving us time to grab a light breakfast and finish our coffee in peace). And an extra bonus, because of the lack of progesterone, we're able to calm down quicker! We woke up late but by problem-solving and being able to think quickly on our feet with creative solutions, we get the job done with time to spare! And this is just a hypothetical of how our brains in the follicular phase are *raring and ready to go.*

    If you're an artist dealing with a block, pick up your medium during your follicular phase. The flow might not come back to you right away. In fact, it's more likely to come to you while you're doing something mundane when your brain's bored, like what happens when we're doing the dishes. But looking at your task again will remind your brain that you have a problem to solve; a block to conquer!

If you're a business owner or freelancer up against a rough patch or plateau, get messy with it during your follicular phase. Crack open the spreadsheets or a mind map and play around with your options. *Throw stuff against the wall, and see what sticks!*

If you're a student who just can't seem to wrap your brain around a unit in your lessons, give it another go in your follicular phase! Turn off the distractions, go back to your notes, and let your brain get flexible around the learning block.

By the way, our hormones are not the only factors channeling into these three interconnected superpowers. Our surge in energy and resiliency is fed by the follicular phase's fourth superpower, a superpower that literally *feeds* us!

MICRONUTRIENT ABSORPTION

Ok, so there is far more nuance and juicy complexity behind this superpower that we promise to dig into later when we talk about food. For now, all we need to discuss is that the lining of our guts is covered in a slick of good and bad bugs (bacteria, fungi, viruses, and archaea) called our *gut microbiome*. These good and bad bugs are the newest branch of medical science, and it turns out they do far more than help us digest our food. For example, they also help with hormone creation and breakdown, immune function, skin health, and even how fast we run. To say that our microbiomes do a lot is a huge understatement.

But right now, we're just going to focus on the obvious act of our microbiome: helping us break down our food. In our follicular phase, the relationship between our gut lining, the tissue that helps us absorb nutrients, and our microbiome is even closer and more beneficial than normal. And that's saying something because our gut lining and microbiomes are pretty dang close on an average day.

What this ends up doing is heightening our rate of micronutrient absorption---or, rather, the amount of nutrients we can absorb from any given meal. (And again, we will touch on this more when we talk about food in Chapter 6.) In short, that means eating nutrient-dense foods and beverages during this phase can set our bodies up for success throughout the month. Our bodies seem to expect to stockpile micronutrients during our follicular phase in spades so that later, in the luteal phase when our bodies are less absorbent for micronutrients and our digestion slows down, we can tap into the stores of micronutrients we made during our follicular phase.

The science on this is still very new, so bear in mind that our understanding of how this superpower works is not set in stone. But the short of it is that eating nutrient-dense veggies during the follicular phase can set our bodies up for nourished-success for the rest of the month-ish---more so than if we ate the same foods at any other point in our cycle.

HEIGHTENED IMMUNITY

Our last note about our microbiomes and our follicular phase is supercharged enough that we consider it to be our fifth superpower: our immune systems are *on point*.

Coach Korra likes to liken this superpower to Chris from Parks and Rec who compares his body to a microchip and is told by a doctor that he is the healthiest patient he's ever seen. Well, That's us in our follicular phase! The heightened micronutrient absorption and tight-knit relationship with our microbiomes makes our immune systems near infallible.

Granted, even with this super-boost, our immune systems need the go-go juice of proper self-care, nutritional food, and adequate rest to activate this superpower, but if we provide our bodies with the tools it needs, we won't get sick here! Have you ever noticed that when you come down with a cold it's almost always either followed by or in tandem with your period? That's because during our luteal phases we don't have this superpower, so we become just as prone to illnesses as non-menstruating humans. But during our follicular phase, getting sick is practically a non-issue.

Now, this doesn't mean that we are advocating for anyone to go maskless during a global pandemic or willingly submit themselves to contracting serious illnesses, like mononucleosis or sexually transmitted illnesses (STIs). Instead, we hope this superpower can give you some confidence in all of the unseen ways that your powerful body tells you that it loves you.

We also think it is important to mention how this superpower can sometimes contort itself into a supervillain. Autoimmune conditions arise when our immune systems become extra jacked up and decide to start attacking different parts of our own bodies---something they are not supposed to do---and statistics show that around 78% of people who suffer from autoimmune conditions are AFAB/cis-women.

Why? How? Well, a part of that is because of all the endocrine disruptors and systemic stressors we live with, which are disproportionate in comparison to cis-men in those same environments. But where assigned male at birth (AMAB)/cis-men would generally see their immune systems weaken, a good percentage of AFAB bodies respond by beefing up their immune systems and then sending them out to attack something. The problem is that our immune systems cannot adequately attack systemic sexism, lack of sleep, processed foods, etc., so they end up going a bit haywire and attacking our own tissues.

If you are one of the many people suffering from an autoimmune disease, we have some resources in our back index you may find helpful. Holistic medicine is finding more success with putting autoimmune disorders

Follicular Phase (Pure)

into remission than conventional medicine has been. This is because holistic medicine works with all of the data our bodies receive---food, sleep, movement, stress, etc. Coach TL and Coach Korra are by no means experts on the subject of autoimmune diseases, but we recognize that working to heal your immune system can be an important factor to claiming all of the superpowers your biology would otherwise innately possess.

TECHNIQUE RETENTION

Our last follicular superpower to discuss is that we are *really* good at *learning* and *retaining* new information during our follicular phase, both physically and mentally (Apel, 2017). In a study done on athletes in their mid-follicular and mid-luteal phases, athletes saw a significant increase in torque* when training in their pure follicular phase, versus when they trained in the middle of their luteal phase---where they saw virtually no improvement. This part of our cycle is when our whole nervous system becomes a sponge for new information.

For our musicians and craftsmen, the follicular phase is the best time to tackle that difficult passage, or to work on that tricky part of your current project. Our body's circuitry is all set to retain one hour of practice as if it was two, and to make the hand-eye coordination of detailed craftsmanship work easier to maneuver---even when it's brand new to us. Just like we discussed earlier with our creativity superpower, this technique retention may not click right away, but during your follicular phase that click is easier to reach than two weeks ago when your body was prepping for your period.

For our athletes, this makes the follicular phase the perfect time to work on form. How often have you tried to get the alignment just right on your deadlift so you can hit your best PR? Or been told you need to engage your abs more on that twist or turn? For serious athletes, the follicular phase is the time to focus on your form because your body is more likely to see the route and *remember* the climb.

For our menstruating humans whose movement may be less intense, this superpower is still useful! Have you ever wanted to learn to do a handstand? Or a pistol squat? Or, have you ever wanted to learn to embroider or woodwork? If it's a physical challenge and there's an element of technique involved, the follicular phase is the time to try your hand (or full body) at it. In the example of handstands, your brain will be communicating to your body better which muscles need to engage and where your human hardware needs to hold its weight in space as your senses take in the world from a completely new gravitational direction. Sound like there's a lot involved? There is! During our follicular phase our circuitry is communicating well enough to handle it.

Our follicular phase comes with an increase in estrogen and dopamine, diminished progesterone and cortisol, and a very pleased gut microbiome. All of these factors come together to make for superhuman energy levels, as well as a hyper absorbent body and mind. These changes internally allow us to move through the world with a new energy and vibrancy, it's like when the first buds of spring begin to grow and you feel the warmth right around the corner. Now let's focus on how to channel these benefits.

*Torque is the capability of a force to produce rotation---it is a normal product of the movement that occurs when a bone rotates about the joint.

USING THESE SUPERPOWERS

We've been talking about how to use these hormones as we discuss them---but the follicular phase has **a lot** of superpowers, so if you've felt a little lost keeping up, no worries! We're going to break down some basics of how to utilize your follicular phase to enhance your life.

Overall, our pure follicular phase is the best time to engage with the exciting aspects of a new project: Planning, getting creative with the possibilities, fleshing out details, learning new things, and feeling confident that you can handle the sticky parts when life goes awry.

Unlike during our periods, when our human hardware wants us to slow down and stew in *yin* energy, our pure follicular phase is in alignment with our modern go-go-go lifestyles. The only thing our pure follicular phase asks for in return is support. This means that any boundaries or self-care we might have realized we need during our periods, *need* to be implemented during our follicular phase. If we realized that we are burnt out because we stay up all night binging TV shows, we can't keep engaging in that self-harming habit and expect our follicular phase to offer up the very best superpowers it has to offer.

We're superhumans, but that doesn't mean we don't need support.

For some people this may mean crowding out sugary foods with more leafy greens and complex grains during their follicular phase (more in Chapter 6). For others this might mean wiggling their bodies more frequently throughout their day. And for some folks, it may mean making sleep more of a priority. The follicular phase comes with some great powers, and like Spider-Man's Uncle Ben once said, "With great power comes great responsibility" (Raimi 2002). And in this instance, we would like to add: a great responsibility to take care of ourselves.

TL;DR
FOLLICULAR PHASE (PURE)

- » Our pure follicular phases are full on *DO*-ing energy
- » The superpowers of our pure follicular phase are:
    - ~Energy
    - ~Stress resistance
    - ~Heightened mood
    - ~Heightened planning, creativity, and problem solving
    - ~Increased micronutrient absorption
    - ~Heightened immunity
    - ~Technique retention
- » "With great power comes great responsibility" **to take care of ourselves.**

Chapter 4
Ovulation
(The Event)

Ah, ovulation---the only day of the month-ish when our bodies are fertile!

Oh, did you not know? There is only *one* day out of our *entire* cycle when it's possible for us to become pregnant.

During ovulation, one (or both!) of our ovaries release an egg and it floats through the connected fallopian tube, only to disintegrate about 24 hours after leaving its ovary. The existence of this egg outside our ovaries is what makes us fertile, so it's only for 24 hours after it pops free that we can fertilize that egg. Granted, sperm can live for up to five days within the human uterus, so it's inaccurate to say that conceiving can only happen on the day of ovulation---but, we still think it's important to highlight just how small our fertility window is.

Additionally, much like our periods, which have been phased out of the medical vernacular from being called a "hormonal phase," ovulation is no longer considered a hormonal or ovarian phase of our cycle. And for that purpose, much like with menstruation, we like to refer to it as an *event* of our cycles. (Flip back to page 23 for the difference in uterine and ovarian cycles.)

Despite ovulation no longer being considered a hormonal phase, the superpowers associated with it do come from our hormones. Before or during ovulation, estrogen---which has been climbing all throughout the follicular phase---finally peaks! As it does, we get the tiniest little bump of testosterone to go with it---the only time we make more testosterone---and, from what science can tell us so far, these two hormones are what give us our ovulation superpowers (refer to the chart on page 43).

Across our research, we have found a myriad of differences in what is actually happening to us hormonally during ovulation. Some sources say these hormones peak before we ovulate, others say they peak *as* we ovulate, and one source said that we completely break them down by the time we ovulate. We'd like to remind you that there are *loads* of discrepancies in our hormonal research and data because we simply aren't studied enough, and---as Maya Dusenbery's Doing Harm (2018) points out---there are huge hormonal and biological differences from menstruating human to menstruating human that our cis-male-centered science still hasn't figured out how to work with.

With all of that in mind, we ask that you take the time to tune in to *when* your ovulation superpowers hit you. They might not hit their highest potency when your cervical mucus or period tracking app tells you you're ovulating, but that doesn't mean that you won't get these super juicy superpowers at some point during, or around, your actual ovulation.

Some folks might think ovulation is the least attractive part of our cycles because they are the *one* day when we could be at risk of conceiving. But, for anyone who has even an inkling of that sentiment, we ask you to reconsider. Because when it comes to our ovulation's superpowers, "attractive" is the best word to describe them.

ATTRACTIVE

You may have perked up a little at this idea that we are quantifiably more attractive during a certain point of our cycles. Well, we're happy to say that it's totally true! Granted, beauty is always in the eye of the beholder! But the changes our human hardware undergoes during ovulation is biologically hardwired into the human race to make us appear more attractive.

For starters, our faces become more symmetrical during ovulation. It's not a *huge* difference, but it's enough to garner more friendly attention than we might be used to during the rest of the cycle. Why does this make us more attractive? It's theorized that symmetrical faces convey proper nutrition as a youth, and therefore a healthy individual. Some research has even shown that most models are perceived as "beautiful" because they tend to have more symmetrical faces than the average population. When we ovulate, our facial symmetry moves the needle *just a touch* closer to "mirror image."

Secondly, our voices go up in pitch. Like with facial symmetry, it's just a touch higher, but to folks who are sexually attracted to fem-bodies, that slight touch of change is enough to make an attraction difference in their subconscious.*

The third factor is *pheromones* that we release through our skin and sweat. Research has shown that our sweat during ovulation smells *attractive* to straight cis-men,** versus when we are actively bleeding and our sweat just smells like sweat. The researchers attributed it to pheromones in our sweat that told potentially interested partners that we were fertile. And indeed, if during ovulation you walk into a room of folks who'd be interested in your biology, be prepared for heads to turn your way---these pheromones work subconsciously, but they *work!* And it turns out, this pheromone difference works both ways, too!***

Menstruating humans are more attracted to their partner's/potential partners' sweat when they're ovulating, and perceive their partner's/potential partners' sweat to just smell like sweat when they're menstruating. In a room full of folks all looking to date each other, the pheromones of menstruating humans are the orchestrators of "who's going to be into who" because we are the only demographic whose biology and fertility is changing from week to week.

The study was done exclusively on cis-men and cis-women, but we hypothesize it's totally possible for those pheromones to work outside of heteronormative attraction.
**Because the study was only conducted on cis-women, this attraction-bonus may not show up in folks on Testosterone.*
***Unrelated to ovulation, but this pheromone thing also makes us disgusted by the smell of family members' sweat, or folks who are genetically similar to us. Turns out, nature's not into incest, and uses these pheromones as one of the barriers to reproducing within our own family tree. How cool is our biology?!*

SOCIABILITY

Along with turning us into a shining beacon for attention, ovulation also changes our brains to be more adroit at socializing, equipping us with the skills to handle that uptick in attention. Coach Korra calls this the time of the "social savant," but truthfully, we're just better at reading social cues and navigating social situations with more ease. We're more likely to make a well-delivered joke to ease tension, or to read between the lines of someone's super subtle body language. We don't all reach the same level of social skills, but we do all get a pretty mighty boost!

Adding fuel to the sociability fire, Alissa Vitti of FLO Living has unearthed research about how, during our ovulation events, the pleasure centers of our brains light up from the mere act of talking. So not only are we far more socially skilled when we ovulate, but socializing, connecting, and communicating verbally also bring us *joy!* For introverts like Coach Korra, this superpower can be a huge leg up in a world that rewards outgoing personalities. And for extroverts like Coach TL, this superpower is the time to *thrive* in your element and lavish in all that sociable joy!

ORGASMS

Did you know that the distance between your clitoral gland and the vaginal canal can increase the ease with which a person can orgasm? It's not a hard and fast rule, but in general, the closer the clitoral gland is to the vaginal canal, the easier, or faster, a body can reach orgasm. And guess what? When we ovulate, our clitoral glands move closer to our vaginal canals. This may not translate so directly to folks experiencing bottom growth from hormone replacement therapy (HRT). And for everyone else imagining a massive rearrangement of your sexual organs, don't worry. The distance travelled is at most a few mere centimeters, but those few centimeters are all it can take to make a huge impact in our sex lives. There's not all that much room down there to begin with, so a few centimeters can change a lot!

This is super important when we talk about the orgasm gap, a term used to describe the disproportionate rate of orgasms in heterosexual relationships, with reports saying that cis-men orgasm 91% of the time, and cis-women reportedly only orgasming 39% of the time, and that rate decreases even less for first time hook ups (cis-women only orgasming 7% of the time). An old standard would decry that it's cis-women's fault that we can't orgasm, but in first time hook ups between same-sex female couples, an orgasm happens 64% of the time. That's more than half of the time, meaning the orgasm gap is probably more *cultural* than it is *biological*---despite what cultural stereotypes might say.

And we know that's a lot of stats to throw at you, but we reference all of them to lead up to this one very important point: if you are one of the many, many menstruating humans who doesn't orgasm with your partner, it is *not* a mistake of your human hardware. Our beloved biology wants us to orgasm so badly that it changes every month to make reaching orgasm easier! If you think you might be a part of the orgasm gap statistic, check out some of the enlightening resources on sex education and sexual pleasure in our resources section. You and your beautiful body deserve orgasms.

At this point you might be noticing a theme with all of the ovulation's superpowers: *sex*. And you're not wrong; the majority of ovulation's superpowers are related to calling on and engaging with a mate---it is, after all, the *one* day in our entire cycles when we're fertile. But for our asexual fam and *everyone* who's not here to learn about baby-making, we have good news: not *all* of ovulation's superpowers are geared towards reproduction.

APPETITE

Long ago, when we were still evolving and our hormone cycles were the only things telling us to eat and go to bed, our ovulation event was probably a pretty tricky thing to manage. Do you know how much work it takes to go out and hunt and forage just to have enough to eat for one day? Way back when, food finding took up the vast majority of our time and energy. And while socializing filled in the downtime when spearing fish in the river, taking the time to engage in reproduction took extra time that we might not have had every month.

Now, this is just a theory, mind you, but it's possible that our bodies decided that getting down and dirty with a possible mate during our very short window of fertility was more important than stocking up on extra meals for a possible famine tomorrow. How does this show up today? During our ovulation week our appetite is decreased and our hardware is more apt to burn our own fat stores for fuel. Is it perhaps to give us more time to go flirt with the sexy forager across the fire pit? Or to make us more available to leave our small community and go find a fun-buddy in a neighboring cave? We like to think so.

Either way, the superpower is still there: decreased appetite and a human hardware that is superduper down to use our own fat deposits (stored up energy) as fuel.

INJURY PREVENTION (THIS ONE IS COOL)

Estrogen saves our muscles, tendons, and ligaments from injury! Coach TL likes to point out that all of the above are the "stuff" that connects our body and keeps it in motion. For our visual learners, the best analogy is ombre hair: ligaments are the root that is darker, then the tendons that are lighter, and ending with the muscles which are lightest. Basically, these parts are all made of the same matter and serve different purposes. They all wrap around and protect our joints and bones and set us in motion. And during ovulation, when estrogen peaks, our chances of injuring this matter is minimal.

But wait a minute, estrogen is climbing all through the pure follicular phase, so does this superpower work there, too?

Good catch "imagined voice of our reader", and *yes!* This superpower starts out as a regular power during the follicular phase---not quite superhuman yet---and then during the week of our estrogen peak (ovulation), this power cranks up its potency to 100% and becomes a true superpower.

Do you also remember how in the follicular phase our nervous systems are more attuned and our brains really know where our bodies are in space? Well, like we've explained, ovulation is an *event* of the follicular phase, so this superpower is still active and it only further contributes to ovulation's refusal to injure you. This means we can jump without rolling out weak ankles, and we can wind up a ball without overextending a rotator cuff. It's all good news for an active human hardware---even a human hardware that isn't normally active, but wants to give activity a try. Peak estrogen is the time to take a risk and just go for it!

FOLLICULAR+

Just like we said, ovulation happens *during* the follicular phase. This means that all of the pure follicular superpowers that we talked about in the last chapter *are still present when we ovulate!* Most of the follicular phase's superpowers are based on its rising estrogen, so it's no wonder that during ovulation, when estrogen peaks, we retain most---if not all---of the follicular superpowers! For this reason, we like to say that ovulation is *follicular+*.

This means that all of the *do*-energy, and all of the creativity and problem-solving superpowers that we can harness during the follicular phase, stays with us during ovulation. We can *DO* so much that we enter into *GIVE*-energy. The only caveat is that during ovulation our brains can be *so* hungry for socializing that some of the more quiet and thoughtful superpowers of the pure follicular phase might be harder to utilize. For example, sitting down to brainstorm about your next novel might feel uninspiring if you're doing it alone, or only on paper. Whereas talking it through with someone, or brainstorming aloud into a tape recorder may be more your speed here. But that doesn't change the fact that they are there, at our disposal, should we need them.

RISK-TAKING

Our last superpower of the follicular phase is our favorite; we think it's the most badass of them all. It's risk-taking.

Between the social skills boosting our popularity temporarily, the supreme injury prevention, and energetic confidence from all of the follicular phase's superpowers, our ability to take big risks has a greater chance of paying off. Therefore, this is the time to do the things that scare us. It is the perfect time to push yourself physically, mentally, and socially. Our human hardware is equipped to take on the challenge and see us through to new goals. For example, I (Coach TL) am an aerialist. During ovulation each month, I schedule in training time to master a new skill in the air or on the ground that has been out of reach previously---such as a dragon squat or a new drop on the trapeze. This is the time where we can not only master these skills, but we are also least likely to get injured. Why not go BIG?!

The thing about risk-taking is society has conditioned us to be the folks who are steady and practical, while cis-men are encouraged to take on the risk . . . . We say the heck with that. Go against the grain. Take your innate superpowers that surface every month and channel them into feats of strength, courage, and gumption. Ovulation is a time to DO, and then GIVE. You're filled with hormones post-ovulation, and this abundance encourages us to say YES! To *everything*. Anything feels possible, and this is a wonderful time to share this exuberant energy with the world.

ASK THE WORLD FOR THE IMPOSSIBLE

Between the heightened social skills, boosted follicular superpowers, and subconscious attractiveness, it's hard to imagine that we wouldn't be able to hold sway over anyone we give our attention to during our ovulation event. And it's for this reason that we like to say, *ask the world for the impossible; we're more likely to get it.*

Ovulation is the time to do the things that would normally have us blushing and stammering our way through---asking for a raise, asking someone out, setting boundaries, convincing someone to your way of thinking, or even asking a group of people to invest in you! Things that seem insurmountable, or that trigger our imposter syndrome, deserve a mindset shift here in our ovulatory event because we become more enigmatic and magnanimous to the outside eye---*people want to please us.* So we say, ask them for what you want---even if it seems impossible! The world is so vehemently on our side during ovulation.

Ask the world for the impossible; you're more likely to get it.

TRACKING

When do I ovulate? We get this question all the time, especially from folks eager to harness their ovulation's superpowers to achieve something fantastic. But the answer to that is tricky because, as usual, it's different for everyone. And more than that, if the confusion in science is any indication, your actual ovulation event might not sync up to when you get your superpowers.

First, our estrogen spikes. This tells our targeting hormone, luteinizing hormone (LH), to crank up the heat and cook our egg for ovulating. The peak of estrogen and testosterone give us the magic to start the process, but it's the LH that actually triggers our ovulation event. Because of this, it's very possible that some of us are hitting peak ovulation superpowers (from the increase in estrogen and testosterone) before we actually produce an egg.

We are huge proponents of hormone tracking. Keeping up with where you are in your cycle is how you can lean into the superpowers before they even make their presence known. But when it comes to ovulation, we have to advocate for a little extra work with *self-awareness*.

We first recommend getting your hands on a cycle-tracking method---selfishly we would love you to use The Superpowers Planner (the paired planner to this book) but if an app is more your style, there are loads to choose from. Coach Korra has used Flo, but finds Tia to be the most holistic (and funny). She currently uses The Superpower Planner along with Natural Cycles because it's the only FDA-approved algorithm-based contraceptive. Coach TL loves a physical planner---therefore The Superpowers Planner is her go-to, but don't be afraid to try each one to find out which works best for you!

The alternative to app trackers is to track via your cervical fluid, which some folks find easier to manage than apps, and for our genderqueer friends, it can be less triggering seeing how most apps are highly gendered. However, some folks (like Coach Korra) find tracking via cervical fluid near impossible due to issues like an inconsistency in vaginal lubrication/discharge---so choosing one method or the other, or even using both, is perfectly *OK!* For folks who aren't concerned about pregnancy (such as those in a same sex couple), you might even find it most helpful to only track your symptoms and energy throughout your cycle. Again, so long as what you're doing works for you, there are no wrong answers; *it's your body.*

Textbook ovulation happens at the halfway point between two periods, but some folks might find that they naturally ovulate on day 10 of a 28-day cycle, or day 18 of a 30-day cycle. Either way, you will most likely notice your superpowers present themselves half a week before your estrogen peaks around ovulation, and say good-bye half a week later. Even though ovulation only lasts for 24 hours, the superpowers we're interested in generally stick around for a full week straddling our estrogen peak.

The importance of tracking your ovulation is that this event will determine how long your follicular and luteal cycles last. We all know when we are and aren't bleeding, but the follicular phase doesn't stop until ovulation happens; the luteal phase, likewise, doesn't begin until ovulation is over. The blood-free phases and events to our cycle are scheduled in accordance to ovulation, and ovulation happens at a slightly different time for everyone.

Once you've tracked to the point where you generally know when your phases, events, and different superpowers present themselves, you'll be able to *plan* your time/life in accordance to your cycles. And that's when the real magic happens!

TL;DR:
OVULATION (THE EVENT)

- » Ovulation is full of GIVE-ing energy
- » Ovulation is when an egg is released from one (or both!) ovaries.
- » We are only fertile for 24 hours.
- » The ovulation event doesn't always line up to the peak in our ovulation superpowers.
- » Our ovulation superpowers:
    - ~Everything from the follicular phase
    - ~Increased attractiveness visually, audibly, and through pheromones.
    - ~Heightened social skills
    - ~Easier/quicker orgasms
    - ~Increased injury prevention (thanks estrogen!)
    - ~Primped and primed for risk taking!
- » Ovulation is the time to ask the world for the impossible; *you're more likely to get it.*

Chapter 5
Luteal Phase

Hooray! We've made it to the last phase in the cycle! The luteal phase! This is usually our longest phase, and is the only time when progesterone gets to run the show.

Progesterone, if you recall from our intro on hormones, is a precursor to the stress hormone cortisol and is known for the way it triggers our metabolism to rise. It also helps our uterine lining become lush and thick for a potentially fertilized egg. If you'll also recall, human pregnancy is *such* an intensive and energy-consuming process that our bodies would rather play it safe in every facet possible, so the luteal phase is when our bodies more or less *expect* to be pregnant. One of the ways it does this is by creating the lush uterine lining with the help of progesterone so that, on the off chance that we *did* get busy with a super cutie, the fertilized egg won't *burrow into*, and potentially *through*, our uterus. (Fertilized eggs can be real a-holes.) So our body makes a super thick lining that is designed to be temporary if need be, thus our ability to shed it.

Yeah, yeah, you might be thinking, *that's all the stuff my high school health class actually did cover. Tell me something new!*

Gladly! We like to consider the luteal phase as having three parts to it.

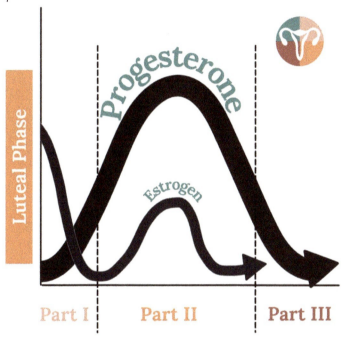

Part I straddles the line between luteal and ovulation. Progesterone is just starting to increase in potency. And depending on where your estrogen peaks in relation to your ovulation event, you could still be breaking down estrogen well into your luteal phase, carrying over some ovulation superpowers.

Part II is when progesterone peaks. Estrogen gets built up into a mini-bump under progesterone's swell, but it is *nothing* compared to the estrogen peak during ovulation. And because progesterone is so dominant, estrogen doesn't get to flaunt its stuff like it can in the follicular and ovulation stages. This part of the luteal phase is when the luteal superpowers are the most potent---coincidentally, this is also when most folks experience premenstrual syndrome (PMS). But don't worry, we'll talk about how PMS can happen when the luteal phase goes awry later.

Part III is roughly three days before our periods, when estrogen and progesterone have, ideally, been broken down into nearly nothing. This lets testosterone, which hasn't budged since being broken down after its teeny tiny bump in ovulation, be the unsuspecting ruler of the roost.

Even though the luteal phase comes in three parts, overall it is considered the *progesterone dominant* phase. And because of progesterone's diva attitude, our luteal phase is where we completely diverge from cis-male-based science and scientific studies---*especially* when it comes to exercise (but we'll talk more about that in a bit). Let's switch tracks for a moment.

In Chapter 2, we talked about how our bodies and brains want to luxuriate in a slower, more spacious space. Then in the follicular phase, we talked about how our energy compass switches into something akin to *yang* energy, which ramps up and keeps ramping up until it peaks in the ovulation event. Well, when we're in our luteal phase, the dial slowly returns back to the internalized energy of the menstrual event.

Sounds like a natural cycle, right? Waxing and waning into each component, repeating certain highs and lows regularly. We see the same model in the change of seasons and even the life cycle of plants. And it should be no surprise! We are creations of nature, after all.

But we don't really live in a natural world anymore. We live in a world built for, and largely designed by, cis-men who haven't been responsible in polling any other demographics for input. And if you're in a highly Westernized world---or worse, America---the idea that we should always be able to emulate the energizer bunny and *go, go, go* every day without fail is the bare minimum of what's expected of you. But the luteal phase doesn't groove to that beat.

Before we get into how and where we need to diverge from the cis-male path to take care of our menstrual bodies, let's talk about the uplifting gifts the luteal phase provides: the superpowers.

TASKMASTER

If, in the luteal phase, we try to live as recklessly and as fast-paced as the follicular and ovulation stages ask for, our bodies will easily take that extra progesterone that is circulating around and turn it into the stress hormone cortisol. As in, we will have *extra* cortisol on top of whatever cortisol our body would have made. In studies on menstruation humans (There are a few that focus properly on us, thank goodness!), researchers found that our resting cortisol rate was the same in the luteal phase as it was in the follicular phase, despite the stressors feeling more . . . well, stressful in the luteal phase. What is actually happening is that when we come up against stressors in the luteal phase, even small ones, we have a much larger cortisol spike/reaction to a stressor that in our follicular phase might feel like no big deal. Aka: stuff stresses us out more in the luteal phase. But don't worry, this isn't a foregone conclusion!

In parts I and III of this phase, our brains are starved for dopamine-boosting estrogen, meaning we need to work a little harder to make small happy sparks in our brain chemistry. And something that can immediately make us feel good is *finishing* tasks; feeling like we're consistently accomplishing things.

Essentially, our brains are easily addicted to productivity in our luteal phase, and this makes us a *taskmaster.*

» Need gas in the car? Done---cue hit of happiness that gives you the energy to do the next thing!
» Need to take the trash out? Check---cue hit of happiness to build off of what you did before!
» Emails piling up? All answered---cue big hit of happiness that can make us feel unstoppable!

Are these *exciting* activities? No, they're not. But in the luteal phase, they're exactly what the doctor called for! A part of this taskmaster superpower of the luteal phase is that we can find magic in the mundane here. And this doesn't only apply to parts I and III of our luteal phase.

In part II of our luteal phase, where estrogen is creating a mini-peak (but progesterone is loudly, and proudly, running the show) our taskmaster skills are especially present. Why? Well, progesterone, as we've mentioned, is a precursor to the hormone *cortisol*, and *cortisol* is a stress hormone. Stress hormones can chill out easier if we have an ample supply of happy hormones and some semblance of stress management techniques at our disposal. Ticking off tasks, while giving our brains doses of happiness, also gives us a sense of control and capability.

There's nothing as overwhelming as an endless to-do list, so by leaning into our taskmaster skills here, that beast of a to-do list can be far more manageable, and even enjoyable, to tackle. Heck! Cross off "to-do" and make it "to-done!"

We'll talk more about how to support our bodies through the stress-factor of our luteal phase in a bit. But for now, it's helpful to know that because of the specific hormone cocktail bathing our brains in this phase, we are far more likely to find awe in the ordinary and to feel both nourished and satisfied from the simple act of *finishing tasks*---no matter how small or how boring they might seem.

STAMINA

The luteal phase is also characterized by something we like to call *staying power*. Another facet of this heightened-cortisol response is that our brains are set up to succeed where continued work is required. We view this as a gift because everything worth doing takes time and *work*, and during the luteal phase---part II especially---that *work* is exactly where our superpowers lie.

What do we mean by "continued work"? Let's say that within her cycle, Coach TL works on a dance piece for a concert with her dance company, AbunDANCE. In her follicular phase, she would ideally throw ideas against the wall by stringing movement phrases together with another dancer. In the week of her ovulation event, she would teach the piece to the rest of her dance company and collaborate with them to make it shine. Then comes the luteal phase, where she would rehearse and run it with them again and again until it was performance-ready.

The luteal phase is when that sustained energy that we all need to reach a goal becomes our biggest asset. We've got more *stamina* and *stick-to-it-iveness*. During the luteal phase, the dial that determines where our energy is directed starts turning inward, making self-projects and *nose-to-the-grindstone* kind of work our forte!

In the follicular phase, our brains are hungry for new information, and we are stewing in a delicious mess of creativity. When our brains are buzzing like this, doing the mundane tasks we all need to do---like say, getting our taxes done---are really hard to focus on! Whereas in the luteal phase, sitting down to do our taxes is easier. And every time we finish a "step" on Turbotax our mood lifts, and we feel rewarded.

The luteal phase is a time of TAKE-energy. And it follows after the time to give, therefore we are replenishing the stores. It has the least exciting superpowers, but they're the most *necessary* superpowers to achieve anything worth working towards. Our superpower is the ability to do the work!

USING THESE SUPERPOWERS

If you're still a little dazed by all of the shiny superpowers of the other phases, let us give you some examples of how to use the luteal phase's mundanely magical assets:

- » Clean up your home or Marie Kondo your life
- » Rearrange furniture so it caters more to your needs
- » Hang shelves or finally build that IKEA furniture you bought
- » Schedule your travel plans; build the itinerary
- » Order pantry items for the month
- » Rehearse or practice something
- » Connect the dots in a sporadically written piece you've been working on
- » Organize and declutter your workspace
- » Focus on admin tasks if you run a business
- » And hand in your taxes

If it's a long project you've already started, or something boring that you kept putting off earlier in your month-ish, then it's the perfect task to tackle in your luteal phase---you'll have the right *oomph to* get it done.

SUPPORT

OK, now for the serious part because the luteal phase is where our cycle gets a little messy. Like we mentioned before, the luteal phase is when we completely diverge from almost everything that works for the all-studied cis-man.

For starters, our metabolism increases, raising our core body temperature slightly and demanding more fuel in the form of food and sleep. But at the same time, both our ability to sweat to cool down and our circulation to our outer extremities decreases. This leads to a really warm core but freezing hands and feet. And in case you didn't know, if humans have cold hands and feet, our brains think that we must be cold---so we walk around shivering, grumbling about office temperatures set for the needs of middle-aged white men in suits. But as soon as we do get our hands on a jacket or sweater, we overheat because our core temperature is raised and we can't cool ourselves down by sweating.

Does that chain of events sound familiar? Yeah, it does for us, too.

Let's back up and zero in on one part of that unsatisfying cycle, *we need more fuel.* Both in the form of more sleep and more food. And just to put this into perspective, on any old day, we already need (on average across persons) 25 more minutes of sleep than is recommended for cis-men. And in our luteal phase, we need anywhere from 50-500 extra calories a day (depending on how much work your human hardware does). This is due to a difference in physiology---AMAB have around 4% essential body fat, while AFAB have around 12% essential body fat, because we are designed to reproduce. Have you ever noticed that you feel more tired before your period? Or that you get those all-notorious cravings for high-calorie foods? Folks who experience PMS, have you noticed that your PMS could be classified as extreme hanger?*

Folks, the code to fixing the worst time in our cycles has already been cracked: our bodies have been demanding exactly what they needed all along. Fresh double-blind studies (Legitimately done on us! Yay!) about PMS clearly pointed to inadequate food intake during our luteal phase. It turns out that we need *complex carbohydrates* and *protein* during our luteal phase (And far less of an emphasis on fats. We'll talk about all of this more in-depth in our Chapter 6). And, when we don't get the amount and type of fuel we need, our starving body demands something it can break down fast. Thus comes all of the "unhealthy" cravings we associate with our luteal phase. It's not that we *need* Doritos, it's that we need *more food, period!*

Unfortunately, the common cravings (fast-acting or processed fuel) are not the most supportive fuel for our human hardware during this phase. When we consume foods higher in simple sugars and low in fiber (foods more likely to make our blood sugar spike, called *high-glycemic foods*), our blood sugar goes haywire. On top of the heightened cortisol reaction, we are also more insulin-resistant in our luteal phase. The quick-fix craved foods often create a hormonal cascade that can have us sobbing into pillows like when Cinderella was told she couldn't go to the ball, or rage-screaming like the Queen of Hearts.

In short: you might just need to eat more good food. But what is *"good" food*, you ask? Let's dissect that together in the next chapter.

*Hanger is hungry-anger. The anger we feel when we're hungry. Fun fact, hanger is fully supported by science. It's not all in your head, it's actually about what's missing from your plate.

TL;DR:
LUTEAL PHASE

- » Luteal Phase is an act of TAKE-ing energy
- » The luteal phase has three parts to it
    - ~Part I: low progesterone and either low or decreasing estrogen (depending on your ovulation).
    - ~Part II: progesterone peaks and estrogen has a mini-bump.
    - ~Part III: ideally, progesterone and estrogen break down and are less concentrated than testosterone.
- » The luteal phase is ruled by progesterone, and that's what makes it completely different from the rest of our cycle, and also makes us completely different from the expectations set for cis-men
- » The luteal phase's superpowers are:
    - ~Taskmaster extraordinaire
    - ~Stamina
- » Our luteal phase needs more support than we're taught to give our human hardware, and that's where things go a bit haywire.

Chapter 6
Food

Sometimes it feels like there's an unending back-and-forth between experts on what constitutes "healthy food." Just take eggs for example. At one point, eggs were the epitome of a healthy breakfast, but then we thought they were bad for us, then we thought they were good again. Then we thought the egg yolks were too fatty and harmful, but then we realized the egg yolks are *good* fat and we added them back to the health menu. Now we're discovering that a lot of folks have allergies to eggs, and that they can permeate the gut lining when folks have leaky-gut syndrome, triggering a host of autoimmune issues---so now they're back to waiting in the wings!

Yeah, it's a lot to keep track of.

With this constant back-and-forth between what's healthy and what's not healthy, the only consistent through-line is that whatever the rule proclaims *is not,* automatically works *for everyone.* It should come as no surprise to you at this point, dear reader, that menstruating humans, again, don't get included in much of the prevailing food studies. So it's even more appropriate to hammer in this idea that *no one knows your body like you do*. The newest trend in food science is personalization: figuring out what foods work best for individuals based on their genetics and their *microbiome*. (What is the microbiome? Oh, don't you worry, we will cover that soon!)

When we spoke about the support needs of the luteal phase, we spoke about how we needed more "good food." And both Coach TL and Coach Korra define "good food" as whatever makes you feel nourished and, well, *good!* If gummy bears make you feel happy (emotionally good) but give you a sugar rush (and then crash), they're not a "good food" for your human hardware. If you love the taste of avocado toast but your gut can't happily digest avocados *or* toast, then we don't care how many articles you read about how avocado toast is a healthy dish, it's not a *good food* for *you*. Alternatively, if something makes your human hardware feel energized and happy, but you'd rather spit it out than swallow it, then that's not a good food for you either. "Good foods" sit in the middle of that Venn diagram, in the overlap between what makes your body happy once you've eaten it, and what makes *you* happy to eat!

One of the reasons finding and maintaining a list of "good foods" is so difficult for menstruating humans is that as our bodies and brains change from week to week, so too do our fuel needs. "Good food" to our human hardware is different in our luteal phase than in our follicular phase--- and even different from the ovulation event to the menstrual event. If this sounds overwhelming---*breathe*. We wouldn't bring this up if we didn't have potential solutions to help!

We're going to walk through each of the phases and events of our cycle and give you the broad strokes of which foods can be the most supportive. Think of it like a general guideline, a compass to point you towards different areas of the grocery store (or Seamless/Grubhub's filters). It's not a diet! The rigidity and shame spiraling of diet culture has destroyed many a folks' mental health and bodies for too long and we will not be participating. These are guidelines where you can take what works for you and leave the rest.

But how can we talk about food without talking about diets? Well, as a graduate of the Institute for Integrative Nutrition, Coach Korra is an advocate for a method called *crowding out*. Instead of focusing on the foods to cut *out*, or the limits to what you're "allowed" to eat, *crowding out* focuses on the different types of foods you can call *in*.

With the crowding out method, you might eventually find that you are no longer reaching for unsupportive foods because you've already filled your plate with so many foods that *are* supportive---and then again, maybe not! This is not a race, and the only good grades given out here are determined by your human hardware in the forms of: restful sleep, fast-thinking, long-lasting high energy, and all-around feeling *good* in your human hardware. That's our idea of healthy and supportive eating.

When it comes to discovering what's *good* for *you*, it isn't a destination. Eating well is a journey.

Before we dive into the different phases, let's circle back to that little word we dropped without explaining--- *Microbiome*.

ONE OF THE THINGS THAT MAKES US SO SUPER

Have you heard about the microbiome? It's a buzzword these days in the wellness community, a short-term for our *gut* microbiome. We do have a microbiome on every surface inch of our bodies, but when people say "microbiome" in most health spaces, they mean the one in our gut. A microbiome is a vast network of trillions of cells composed of bacteria, fungi, viruses, and even archaea. In our gut, they line the inner tubing of our GI tract (which our bodies perceive as *outside* of our bodies. Fun fact, your body doesn't think the stuff you ate is inside your body. As far as your body is concerned, that piece of bread you ate for lunch, sitting in your stomach, is outside your body until it's broken down into its smaller components and crossed the lining of your small intestine!).

As of 2021, we have *barely scratched the surface* of understanding the gut microbiome, but so far our understanding has earned it the nickname of the "second brain" because it does *so much* when it comes to directing our bodies. (Newer research is even leading some experts to call it the "first brain," in fact, just to exemplify its importance.) How is that possible? Well, for starters, the gut microbiome carries at least ten times more DNA than we do in our own cells. Heck, there are even more *cells* in our gut microbiome than there are in our own tissues. Some experts joke that we aren't humans walking around with a microbiome, but that we are a microbiome being carried around in a human.

We know, it's a pretty trippy concept.

Our gut microbiome talks directly to our brain via the vagus nerve (and less directly through other pathways), and so far, studies are showing that it's a two-way street. When we feel emotions, they can inform our guts to do certain things---slow digestion, cramp up, give us butterflies---and vice versa; our guts can inform our brains to create certain emotions. That's where some of our chocolate and sugar addictions come into play, by the way. They create an effect in our gut microbiomes that tells our brain to make more happy hormones. Only with sugar, it's not long-lived.

Our microbiomes also influence how much body fat we store and how fast we can run. And, it's even been theorized that not only does it *make* the hormones that direct our menstrual cycles, but the microbes inside of our guts were how we first *learned* to make the hormones that direct our menstrual cycles. The newest studies on this baby field in science are pointing towards our microbiomes being intrinsically and intimately linked to our menstrual cycles. This suggests, in theory, (and works in practice) that changing our food habits to support whatever our human hardware deems as "good," can nix a whole category of menstrual cycle problems: PMS, PCOS, and even endometriosis! And the reach of our microbiome doesn't stop there!

For a more in-depth look on the relationship between microbiomes and vaginal health, check out "#83: Your Gut Microbiome & Your Vaginal Health" (and their relation) in The Period Party *with Nicole Jardim.*

IMMUNITY

When you think of your immune system, what do you think of? Maybe the first thing that comes to mind is your white blood cells and antibodies; both are essential parts of our immune system. But did you know that our body's first line of defense is our microbiomes?

When we eat something, touch something, or breathe in something, that *something* comes in contact with the network of microbes that lives across every surface of our bodies. Eating something would involve the mouth and gut microbiomes (they're different!), touching something would involve different parts of the skin's microbiome (it's different across every area of your body!), and breathing in something would involve the microbiomes in our nose and on the surface of our lungs. We even have a *highly functional* microbiome inside of our vaginas.

If you're someone who experiences chronic yeast infections, that is a sign that your vaginal microbiome is struggling to stay balanced. And, fun fact, one of the biggest attackers to our vaginal microbiome is glycerin, which breaks down into sugar and feeds the yeast fungal cells and nonoxynol (N-9), a common spermicide that is known to

damage vaginal (and rectal) cells. Both materials, by the way, are used in conventional condoms (Horton 2021)!*
All across our different microbiomes, these microbes like having a home---that's us---so they fight off anything disruptive to keep that home and their community of microbes safe. *That's* our first line of defense!

Inside of our guts, our microbiomes are in very tight contact with the cells and tissues of our own bodies. Two of the jobs of the gut microbiome are one: to break down the food we eat and then feed it to us via our intestinal lining, and two: to look out for foreign invaders (*pathogens*) and alert the cells of our immune system when it spots something. In fact, we have a *massive* number of lymphocytes (headquarters for our immune system) lining our large intestine. The food we eat closely corresponds with how our immune system is functioning.

Do you remember one of the superpowers of our follicular phase: *heightened immunity*? There isn't a ton of research to support this (what else is new?), but there *is* a ton of research that shows that the majority of folks with autoimmune conditions were born female. (Not solely menstruating humans, because this affects post-menopausal and pre-menstrual folks as well.) Autoimmune conditions, by the way, are what happens when an individual's immune system gets confused and starts attacking the tissues and cells of their own human hardware.

The best theory we've come across is that our already heightened, and possibly in-flux, immune systems find it easier to flip into overdrive when its best buddy, our gut microbiomes, gets out of whack. Another explanation is that because AFAB folks are so disenfranchised by a culture and medical community that don't cater to us (putting our bodies under far more duress than the catered to cis-men), we're more likely to have immune systems that decide to go rogue. We'll talk about this more in our Chapter 9, but having a full "stress bucket" can be the complicated recipe that makes a simple catalyst for a slew of health problems. But, as for the reasons why AFAB folks get diagnosed with more autoimmune conditions than cis-men---as the little girl in that taco commercial once said, "Por que no los dos?" *(Why not both?)*

One of the trippy concepts we introduced with the microbiome was the idea that, to our bodies, the stuff inside of our guts is considered to be the outside world. That makes *food* a potential foreign invader. The rate of food sensitivities and food allergies has been on the rise in the 21st century, as has the rate of autoimmune conditions. The reason why we stopped to talk about the microbiome and immunity when talking about what foods support us in the different phases of our cycle is that they're all linked! Holistic and functional doctors are finding a lot of success in treating autoimmune conditions via diet and lifestyle changes. There is even growing evidence that *anti-inflammatory diets* can put the highly under-diagnosed and painful disease of endometriosis into remission!

Immunity, food, and just general *feeling well* are all interconnected through our gut microbiome.

Now, we're not saying any of this to have you biting your nails over your food choices. If you're a chronic Oreo binge-eater, you're not "destined to develop hypothyroidism" or anything like that. Something we're going to dive into more in our conversation around food is that, despite the fact that we call our bodies "human hardware," they're not machines---at least, not simple ones. Our bodies don't use simple formulas like "Oreos + more Oreos = hypothyroidism." Our bodies don't even use "calories in - calories out = fat gain/loss." We're too complex for that---*especially* when we bring in the awareness that our microbiomes, the inherently complex and diverse network of microbes inside of our digestive tracts, are probably running the whole show.

Food

OK, cool, you may be thinking. But then, how do I use any of this microbiome information? How does this help me?

The short answer is: by tending to your microbiome. Treat it with care and it will return the favor.

See our list of resources in the back for vagina pH-friendly condom brands.

MICROBIOME CARE

We want to reiterate that microbiome science is still in its infancy, however, there are a few pillars of actionable wisdom we can reasonably rely on when it comes to taking care of our microbiomes.

STEP 1: MAKE PEACE WITH YOUR TUMMY BUGS.

Antibiotics, much like vaccines, are a medical marvel. Diseases that would once slaughter whole cities of people were rendered to mere sniffles that we can shrug off in a week because of antibiotics. But we humans have yet to heal from the trauma bacteria brought us. We use antimicrobials in excess as if sterile environments will allow us to thrive, opting for hand sanitizer and harsh cleaners whenever they're presented to us. But the discovery of our microbiomes help us bring to light a new mindset: that not all microbes are bad, and that living in harmony with microbes can enhance and diversify our microbiomes, making them stronger and more robust against foreign invaders.

One of the things science first got wrong about the microbiome was that it consisted of a binary of "good" and "bad" bugs and that these bugs would battle each other until one side won. But it turns out, that much like a thriving community, a healthy microbiome is nuanced and *diverse* in its entirety. Where science sits now, there aren't "good" or "bad" bugs. Rather, a healthy or unhealthy microbiome relies on the *net* good or *net* bad of all of the relationships and transactions between all of its residents. And one of the biggest factors we're learning to pinpoint as the leading reason for a net good is microbe diversity.

For example, we actually have strains of e. coli in our guts, but because there are only a certain number of them (and because of the interactions they have with their neighbors) they don't usually pose a problem and can even be constructive parts of a healthy microbiome. These are strains of bugs that, if left to their own devices, would land us in the ER. But because the microbiome functions as a community, a healthy microbiome would have a microbe neighbor next to that potential troublemaker to chill them out, or to remind them that they'd be homeless without us to carry them around everywhere.

So where we, in our modern age of hyper-cleanliness, go wrong is in overcleaning, overprescribing, and overeating of antibiotics and antimicrobials. One dose of antibiotics is a nuclear bomb to a complex and highly nuanced system that we rely on for nearly every facet of our existence. Essentially, too many antibiotics can completely wreck a gut microbiome and can easily push a body into a chronic condition like irritable bowel syndrome (IBS).

Now, we're not advocating for living in filth or ignoring your doctor, but there's room for advocacy and choosing more supportive options. You're allowed to talk to your doctor about other forms of treatment that can help protect your tummy bugs, and you're allowed to engage with gentler cleaning products and simpler hand soaps.

Please note, this step is not meant to be used for extreme situations like healing from surgery or fighting off very strong infections.

The last microbiome attacker we want to talk about is meat choice. Most conventionally raised farm animals are pumped full of hormones and antibiotics (to make them grow faster, and because they're fed so poorly their risk of getting sick is incredibly high). If you're reading this, you might already be concerned about the hormones in your meat products, and now we're adding a bit of fuel to that fire because the antibiotics given to that farm animal don't disappear when you stick it on the grill.

But don't worry! We're not advocating for vegetarianism, because just like with medical options and household cleaners, when it comes to your meat products you have *probiotics*. And the options that will protect your tummy bugs are hormone-free and antibiotic free. Sometimes those options are even sitting on the shelf right next to the conventionally raised meats, so you don't even have to go far to find them!

STEP 2: EAT SUPPORTIVE MICROBES.

The more common way to phrase this is to eat *probiotics*. This includes foods like sauerkraut, kimchi, properly pickled pickles, properly pickled *anything*, apple cider vinegar, kefir, raw cheeses, etc. Unlike our skin, nose, and vaginal microbiomes, our gut microbiomes *evolved* to require intentional input from us to give it a consistent influx of new "neighbors." Our skin and nose microbiomes can find new neighbors every time we touch something or take a breath, but our gut microbiomes only encounter new immigrants when we choose to eat something.

And, fun fact, *every culture has some form of probiotic food.* Our ancestors somehow must have figured out that fermenting and pickling foods was something that was great for our digestion and our overall health, which in turn might have been one of the reinforcing factors that made our body's relationship with our gut microbiomes require a constant influx of new microbes. Our gut microbiomes *need* fermented foods in order to thrive!

Something Coach Korra specifically wants to mention regards the fermented drink, *kombucha*. Kombucha has gained a lot of popularity over the past decade so a lot of people who hear "eat more fermented foods" will readily turn to it, but it's not the best option for everyone, and it certainly is not the best option to consistently reach for.

Kombucha is typically high in sugar and caffeine. It makes sense why most people would be on board with a probiotic regiment of kombucha; it fits in pretty well with a lot of the addictions we already have (sugar and caffeine). But unlike the sugar found in fruits and even some veggies, kombucha doesn't come with any fiber to offset how quickly the sugars will hit your bloodstream because it's a drink. And the caffeine? Well, we could go on and on about how we're an over-caffeinated world, but we'll just leave it at that--- we're over-caffeinated and kombucha only adds to that.

Does this mean "never drink kombucha?" Not at all! We're merely advocating that you reach beyond the sugary drink section in your search to find supportive care tools for your gut microbiome. (Be like Buckwheat, in little rascals. "I've got 2 pickles, I've got 2 pickles . . . hey hey!" [Spheeris, 1994].)

STEP 3: EAT THE STUFF YOUR SUPPORTIVE MICROBES EAT.

It makes sense, right? If you want to keep your microbe community happy and humming, you have to give them new neighbors and *stuff to eat*. Every time we take a bite of food, we are feeding the microbes in our gut---but they all eat different things. So every time we take a bite of food, we are feeding certain bugs and starving others--- or rather, we are strengthening certain types of bugs and crowding out other types of bugs.

This is where the science can get really murky because we still don't know enough. The Dental Diet by Dr. Lin (2019) breaks it down really simply: we need to feed the more helpful bugs. Take, for example, that neighbor to e. coli we mentioned above who tells e. coli to *chill out*. We want to feed these supportive microbes so there can always be someone there to tell e. coli to chill out.

And this doesn't just apply to bugs that would keep something serious like e. coli in check. This applies to the bugs that live in our large intestine that have a big say in how much body fat we have, the bugs that are informing our blood sugar mechanisms how to work, the bugs that could be feeding our brain cells dopamine---*everything*.

These foods that, generally, feed our helpful microbes are called *pre*biotics. Prebiotics generally come in two categories:

» Resistant starches: cooked white potato, chicory root, green bananas, and some uncooked grains like oats, etc.
» Fiber: found in abundance in nuts, seeds, leafy greens, veggies, and---while less abundant--- fruits.

Studies on non-modernized cultures found that people were eating, on average, about 28 grams of fiber a day, while the rest of us can barely eat half that amount in a day even if we try really hard. Our modern diets simply don't contain enough fiber---but that's no reason to give up on trying!

Crowding out with fiber would look like incorporating chia seeds into your juice or water bottle, grabbing some walnuts to pair with an apple for a snack, opting for a dark green and full-bodied salad a few more times a week, and maybe even eating the green tops on strawberries! Coach Korra does this and says that they don't change the taste at all!

FOOD FOR MENSTRUATION

Phew! Thank you for sticking with us through our microbiome foundation. If some of the concepts got a little too heady for you, no worries! The summation of all of that was that *the stuff we eat matters.* And now, let's get to the food stuff that supports the most stigmatized part of our month: our periods. And as we go on, try to remember that this is not a diet; call in foods as you see fit and at whatever pace feels manageable for you!

SUPPORTIVE PERIOD FOODS

Ok, so do you remember way back in Chapter 2 when we talked about the little sidekick of a superpower to our periods? How we told you our period blood can fertilize soil? Well, a big part of that is because our period blood is super nutrient-rich. This begs the question that if we are losing a lot of nutrients in our period blood, do we need to replace those nutrients?

The answer is yes! And do you know the one type of food that contains almost all of the nutrients we need to make up for that lining loss, including rebalancing our electrolytes and sodium levels? *Seaweed.*

It turns out, there are tons of different kinds of seaweed: kelp, nori, arame, dulse, and even Irish moss. They'll all jive with your body differently so, if this is the one period food you want to try to call in, we suggest starting small. (And we realize as amazing as it is, it may not be for everyone . . . Coach TL can't get on the seaweed train---her dog nose legit can't handle it.)

Perhaps merely going out for sushi when your bleed comes to call is all you can manage. *Great.*

Maybe you order the seaweed salad while you're there. *Amazing.*

Maybe the next time you're at the grocery store you stop in the Asian seasonings section (that's normally where seaweed lives in mainstream stores) and you bring home a pack of dried seaweed to eat with your next period. *Stellar!*

Most of the time seaweed is sold as a dried snack or in a bag of water because otherwise, it has a shelf-life of less than a day. And as for how to cook it? The possibilities are borderline endless. The book *Eat Like a Fish* by Bren Smith (2019) has some amazing insight on seaweed as a food group, and even comes with a list of recipes developed by high-end five-star chefs from across the globe.

Seaweed has many nutritional benefits. It supports thyroid function, is an excellent source of vitamins and minerals, contains antioxidants, provides fiber and polysaccharides for gut health, curbs appetite, reduces blood cholesterol levels (lowering risk of heart disease), and it improves blood sugar control! WOW!

According to that same book, *Eat Like a Fish*, seaweed was a main food group in the diets of every culture that sprung up near the water, so adding it back into our diets can be immensely beneficial for a lot of us---but not all (Smith 2019). If you're someone whose ancestry hailed from an inland part of the world, you might find that seaweed isn't the Hail Mary it might be for someone whose entire ancestry hails from fisherman stock---and that's OK! Even if you just can't eat seaweed for whatever reason, there are still more foods out there you can incorporate to support a conventionally unsupported time in our cycles.

Our second most helpful food "group" isn't really a food group at all, but a food phenotype: *purple foods*. When we say purple foods, we are including foods that make a purple or deep crimson juice. These foods get their purple color from a particular type of antioxidant that is extremely beneficial in helping our bodies cope with unsupported periods. This includes foods like blueberries, blackberries (remember, the juice is purple!), cherries, pomegranate (deep crimson juice!), purple cabbage, purple peppers, purple potatoes, and even purple string beans. Yes! Purple string beans are a thing! You can get them readily at almost any farmer's stand during string bean season (May to October).

Because this supportive food "group" spans across many different vegetables and fruits, it's easier for folks to find something supportive to incorporate. Maybe you enjoy a handful of fresh blueberries every day of your next period, or you order the purple potato casserole. Either way, choosing the purple, antioxidant-rich food will give your actively bleeding human hardware a bit of an extra *oomph* to juggle all of the biological demands that come from actively bleeding while living in a world that still expects us to adhere to someone else's standards.

We have one more food "group" to introduce as a period support food, and this one brings us back to the sea: *non-fish seafood*. When we say that we mean foods like clams, scallops, oysters, lobster, crab, and even octopus and squid. The soft white meat and lingering remains of the sea in these sea animals helps an actively bleeding body rebalance electrolytes and digest---which is a task most bleeding bodies would rather not expend the energy to focus on when there's more important work to be done.

Speaking of how our bodies aren't always super jazzed about prioritizing digestion during our menstrual events, our final suggestion is a temperature. *Warm foods* are very kind to actively menstruating bodies. When we eat warm foods, our bodies don't have to expend extra energy to warm up our core---as opposed to cold foods that make us feel colder and force our bodies to do the extra work to maintain our temperature. This doesn't have to be applied to everything you eat (none of our suggestions do), and if you're someone who lives in a super warm place and you walk around overheating all the time *anyway*, then this food suggestion might not serve you. But either way, choosing to eat easily digestible foods is a very kind choice to make to support your body while it is actively bleeding.

Fun Fact: The veggie fennel (one of Coach TL's favorite things ever) has analgesic and anti-inflammatory properties that both support and can decrease the length of blood flow during your period.

WHERE PERIOD MEETS FOLLICULAR

If you recall from our breakdown of when our menstrual event begins and ends within the follicular phase, for most of our periods (day three and beyond) our human hardware is straddling both the menstrual event and our follicular phase. When it comes to how to support your body during this time, we recommend the *listening* method ---all you need to do is ask your human hardware, "What do I need?" and listen to what it's asking for. It might be that your periods are so intense that your human hardware is happiest munching on kelp noodles every day that bleeding occurs. It could also be the case that come the 3rd day of your period, your body is just so over the culinary trip to the ocean, and is instead ready to dive into foods that are supportive for your cycle's next focus, the pure follicular phase. Let's talk about what foods those might be.

SUPPORTIVE FOODS FOR THE PURE FOLLICULAR PHASE

The first food group we have to talk about which supports the follicular phase is something we already mentioned when we discussed the microbiome, *fermented foods*. Our immune systems in the follicular phase are working at max capacity, so when we incorporate fermented foods into our follicular meals, our human hardware can ensure that the new neighbors find their proper niches to help make for a more robust and thriving community---thus fending off sickness later in the luteal phase when our immune systems are more prone to burning out.

If we're eating a lot of *pro*biotics, it means we also need to be eating foods that feed those probiotics, also called *pre*biotics! During the follicular phase, which tends to want a lighter load on our plates, foods that are high in fiber, give us a good crunch, and take longer to digest are more supportive---foods like carrots, string beans, bell peppers, or lettuces. You want veggies that come with a satisfying *crunch*. Adding in crunchy veggies here gives our microbiomes food to keep them happy, and the solid shape to crunchy veggies means that our digestive systems can remain full longer---which is a good thing here!

Fun fact about chewing! It's the only way to circulate blood to a certain part of the front of our brain. Chewing is necessary for a thriving brain and digestive system!

Our appetites and metabolisms are much slower during the follicular phase, and this lines up with our need for low-calorie, slow-digesting foods that require some extra elbow grease to break down. Another food group that fits this bill is **slow-burning grains**, like oats, spelt, and whole-grain bread. Having to break down these whole grains takes extra work from our digestive system and creates a slow and steady output of glucose to feed our body's cells, which is exactly what our follicular phase finds supportive to keep our hungry brains steadily fed (so we don't get hangry), and to keep perking up our metabolism.

Another food group we can eat here to help our immune system long after the follicular phase is over is **citrus** foods. Lemons, oranges, limes, and strawberries are all really supportive for our immune systems. And because this phase is so good at stockpiling nutrients to use later, all of the extra immune-supporting nutrients we eat here can be called on later to fend off sickness. Again, *how cool are we*?

The last general food group that's supportive for our human hardware in the follicular phase is foods that are high in **saturated fats**. These are foods like pasture-raised butter, olives, cheeses, whole milk (bonus there for the probiotics!), nuts and nut butters, seeds, and beans. These high-fat foods contain essential fatty acids that allow our human hardware to absorb all of the micronutrients it wants to stockpile. Did you know that fat is necessary for us to absorb micronutrients? So without this healthy-fat intake during our follicular phase, we can be eating all of the veggies and citrus foods we want, but we won't be able to retain much of the micronutrients we manage to break down. This need for fat can be fulfilled by adding a handful of pecans to a navel orange grab-and-go snack, drizzling some extra olive oil over your steamed carrots, enjoying more whole-fat cheese than you normally allow yourself, or by enjoying the dip part of "veggies and dip." YUM!

As with every stage of our cycles, when it comes to food, so long as it makes you feel good during and after eating it, there are no wrong answers.

THE OVULATING BODY

Ovulation is the event in our cycles that does all that it can to make us more attractive and adept with social prowess. And much to the glee of the diet industry, the ovulating body is usually less interested in finding food and more interested in throwing on a sexy outfit and painting the town red. In general, we have less of an appetite during our ovulation event and our bodies are more apt to burn our own fat stores for fuel, meaning we can often forget to eat and our human hardware will keep chugging along like usual.

But this does not mean that intentionally skipping meals is supportive for an ovulating body. We want to be very clear that just because ovulation's relationship to our appearance and nutritional needs are things that are championed by the toxic diet industry, does not mean that ovulating is a free pass to engage with disordered eating. Likewise, if your hormones are relatively balanced and your ovulation event doesn't fit this paradigm of 'the decreased appetite,' your body is *not wrong*.*

The toxic diet industry likes it when we restrict and shrink ourselves, when we eat more guilt and shame than we do nourishing foods that make us *feel good.* Our whole aim for writing this book is to help menstruating humans become more in touch with what makes their unique human hardware feel good so they can ultimately *unleash their superpowers.* So please, dearest, lovely, and soul-deep-beautiful reader, do not take this framework for ovulation support as a tool to beat yourself down. Add in whatever foods feel supportive to your physical, mental, and emotional health, and keep engaging with what nourishes you.

*If you are interested in learning more about disordered eating behaviors and patterns, either for the sake of knowledge, curiosity, or because you are concerned about yourself or someone else, please see our resources section in the back under "Finding Help."

SUPPORTIVE FOODS FOR OVULATION

Ovulation is best supported by nutrient-dense and high-fiber foods. The two biggest food groups that foot this bill are **dark/bitter leafy greens and seeds**.

Dark/bitter leafy greens are foods like arugula, broccoli rabe, watercress, bok choy, rainbow chard, and even dandelion greens (you can pick them straight out of your yard!). Kale and spinach are leafy greens as well, but these two leafy greens are very high in a type of anti-nutrient that, if eaten raw, can negate all of the nutrients you think you're getting on your plate. This makes them less ideal for raw smoothies, but the anti-nutrients can be broken down by simply steaming, cooking, and even massaging the greens.*

Ovulation's need for a lot of nutrients means that foods like green juices and smoothies make for a supportive menu. But since they don't carry much in the way of fiber, we wouldn't recommend *only* eating smoothies and juices. Adding our second supportive food, *seeds*, to smoothies and juices can boost up their fiber content *and* add more micronutrients! Seeds like chia and flax** are a wonderful addition to a bottled green juice. Chia especially will easily turn a quickly-consumed drink into something with more chew to it---some of Coach Korra's clients even like to add it to their water during ovulation for an extra energy boost during long workdays. Other seeds that you can incorporate into your meals include things like hemp seeds, pumpkin seeds**, sunflower seeds, watermelon seeds, and poppy seeds.

The list of foods that are helpful for our ovulation events isn't long, and that's due in part to how energy-efficient our bodies are during ovulation. But it doesn't mean that ovulation is the time to belittle or abuse our bodies. Incorporate the foods that make you feel like a divine being during your ovulation event so you can wield its super-charged powers with an abundance of confidence and grace.

*Massaging kale and spinach is done by adding salt and lemon juice to the greens and literally massaging the greens until they turn a darker color, this darker color indicates that certain structures within the greens have broken down.
**We will be talking about this later in chapter 11, but if you are someone who experiences anxious, acne-ridden, and bloated ovulation events, you may have too much estrogen circulating. In which case opting out of the phytoestrogen foods like flax and pumpkin seeds will help, as will engaging with sesame and sunflower seeds during your luteal phase to help break down the excess estrogen.

WHERE OUR BIOLOGY DIVERGES FROM DIET INDUSTRY

We've touched on this before, but now it's time to hammer home the message: once our progesterone starts climbing during the luteal phase, our bodies have radically different needs than what we consider to be "normal"---especially when it comes to stress, food, and exercise.

Anyone who was raised female can attest to how aggressively the rules of the diet industry are ingrained into our expectations of what we need to look like and what we need to do to get there.

What's that old rule of thumb? *Calories in vs calories out?* Well, it's a completely debunked theory these days. Modern advances in nutrition science have completely destroyed that old phrase that the diet and fitness industries have used to fat-shame and beat folks into submission. While the science behind that phrase has been completely obliterated, most of the (Westernized) world still abides by the harmful, fatphobic notion that if you eat more you'll become fat.

If you're wondering where we're going with this, please allow us a short drumroll because in our luteal phase our bodies *need to eat more food.* Roughly 50-500 extra calories worth of food---not that we are advocating for calorie counting. Instead, we are advocating for the simple rule of *eating more nourishing foods*.

Where our luteal diets quickly turn into spiral-inducing cravings is when we don't eat more of the foods our bodies need. We restrict and deny until suddenly, desperate for fast energy, our human hardware demands a quick energy fix in the form of high-sugar foods and calorie-dense, but nutrient-poor, processed foods. If you remember from our section on what support our luteal phases need to manifest our superpowers, we are more insulin-resistant in our luteal phase, so high-sugar foods are not helpful at all, even if our bodies are screaming for it. And it's from that chronically repeated pattern of restrict-then-crave, restrict-then-crave, that our luteal phases devolve into PMS and other unfortunate ailments. It's the luteal phase gone wrong.

It might sound scary and feel frustrating as all get-out when we're in the throes of that pattern, but there are actually some wonderfully delicious food groups we can eat to support our luteal phases---foods that will halt this pattern and nourish your lovely human hardware so your luteal superpowers can be unleashed!

SUPPORTIVE FOODS FOR THE LUTEAL PHASE

Two of these three food groups fit into the category of *macronutrients*. *Macronutrients* are the three necessary nutrients of *carbs, proteins,* and *fats*. Having an adequate fat intake is always important, but in the luteal phase, our hardware fares much better when we prioritize protein and carbohydrates, specifically **complex carbohydrates**.

Protein is a macronutrient essential for building and repairing our muscles. And the hormone running the show in our luteal phase, progesterone, likes to nudge our human hardware to *break down* our muscle tissue, making us weaker and ruining all of our good *gains*! When we get into movement in chapter 8, we'll talk about how this affects our workouts. But when it comes to food, we say that protein is a good macronutrient to eat more of in order to mitigate some of the muscle-eating effects of progesterone. As well, upping your protein intake can help stave off cravings in that nasty pattern we mentioned earlier.

Coach Korra's body does best with lots of pasture-raised beef in her luteal phase, and Coach TL's human hardware thrives off of impossible meat, ground turkey and wild cod. But since everyone's different, you might find that your human hardware feels at its best when you incorporate lots of different protein-rich lentils, sheep, pork, or seafood as your luteal protein.

The other macronutrient that we cannot highlight enough as being supportive for our luteal phase is **complex carbohydrates**. What makes a carbohydrate complex? There's a more scientific explanation about how many glucose molecules it takes to make a complex carbohydrate, but for our purposes, our definition is *a carby food that takes a long time to break down*. This is in contrast to simple sugars which are readily found in most fruits and candies. The luteal phase finds support in foods like potatoes, fall squashes, rice, and beans. Incorporating extra complex carbs into your luteal phase can look like ordering some steaming home fries or a baked potato, making yourself some fried brown rice, or, Coach Korra's favorite, roasting some kabocha squash!

These complex carbs are supportive for two big reasons. One, they feed our bodies calorie-dense energy *slowly*, so we never have to feel like we're lacking energy and need a fast-acting sugar to hit our insulin-resistant bloodstream. And two, they help to mitigate the heightened stress-response we're prone to in our luteal phase. Remember when we talked about how progesterone, the star hormone in the luteal phase, can quickly be turned into the stress hormone cortisol and lead to a heightened stress response in our luteal phases? Well, when we eat extra complex carbs, our bodies are able to absorb the shock of that extra cortisol easier. We might still have a higher cortisol spike from small stress triggers, but our bodies are able to shrug it off a little easier than if we didn't have the nice cushion of the extra complex carbs.

The third and final group of foods that are supportive to the luteal phase aren't considered a macronutrient, they're **low-sugar fruits** (Sims and Yeager 2016, 156). As menstruating humans, our livers need an extra boost from sugars because we have more limited glycogen stores than dietary science for cis-men dictates. But in our luteal phase, our bloodstream can't handle large amounts of sugar rocking the boat. This is where low-sugar fruits come to the rescue. These are fruits like apples, pears, dates, raisins, and peaches. If altogether this sounds like a fairly mild-tasting mix of fruits, it's because they're low in sugar; they strike the perfect balance of what most bodies find supportive in the tricky luteal phase.

Coach Korra likes to make big meals of potatoes, squashes, pasture-raised beef, and some easier to digest leafy greens (like *collard greens*), during her luteal phase, having snacks like pear chips and apples with peanut butter between meals to keep both her bloodstream and liver happily balanced---but that's what works for *her.* Coach TL is a date and nuts kind of snack queen in her luteal phase. Some folks might find that munching on wasabi peas, canned peaches, or snacking on whole-grain chips between big meals keeps their energy levels solid throughout the day and keeps any cravings at bay. Everyone's different!

FOOD IS NOURISHMENT

It's like we said at the beginning of this chapter, we are not fans of handing people a diet plan and telling them to "make it work." That would be a recipe for disaster, especially because all menstruating humans are so different from each other; there is no way to make one size fit all. Instead, we hope that these general guidelines of different food groups can help give you a starting point for exploration, and discover what makes *your* unique human hardware hum like a newly serviced cadillac.

Maybe you like the examples of what Coach Korra or Coach TL find most supportive for their bodies, or maybe the most helpful course of action for you would be to try to incorporate *one* suggested food group in each phase of your cycle. It can take our bodies *ten years* to figure out how to operate our menstrual cycle, so it's *perfectly OK* if you need to take time to figure out how to support it. Practice makes progress.

> *At the end of the book, we have included both a cheat sheet to remind you of these food groups suggested AND some recipes, made specifically for this book by one of our superpowered menstruating human friends, Chef Julia DeGruchy. We hope they jump-start your journey of unleashing your superpowers, and living your best cyclical lives.*

TL;DR:
FOOD

- » Instead of "dieting," "crowd out" foods that are unsupportive by incorporating more foods that *are* supportive.
- » The gut microbiome is a network of good and bad bugs living inside of us, and taking care of them by eating fermented foods and prebiotic foods is critical for every facet of our health.
- » Supportive period foods include:
  - ~Seaweeds
  - ~Purple foods
  - ~Warm broths and heated food
- » Supportive follicular foods include:
  - ~Grains
  - ~Saturated fats
  - ~Citrus
  - ~Fermented foods
  - ~Microgreens
- » Supportive ovulatory foods include:
  - ~Everything in follicular
  - ~Dark leafy greens
  - ~Green juices and smoothies
- » Supportive luteal foods include:
  - ~Protein-heavy foods
  - ~Low-sugar fruits
  - ~Carbs (preferably from root veggies)
  - ~More carbs

Your Toolbox to Unleash Your Superpowers

Chapter 7
Breathe

As storytellers, we are keenly aware that every puzzle piece fits into a narrative. The data that our cycle regularly gives us contains details that further the plot of our human hardware's story. Furthermore, there cannot be a story unless we BREATHE life into it; that's where this essential function of our human hardware comes into play. For a process that is so necessary, we as a population have forgotten its nuance and art. In order to unleash the power of our cycle, this key element (oxygen and carbon dioxide), must be addressed and utilized. The research done on breathing techniques (alone, not for menstruating humans) is extensive and, in turn, has found that to truly reap the benefits of our SUPERPOWERS, our approach to breathing is important and highly specific.

The hormone progesterone specifically affects breathing. During the later days of our cycle, 15-28, progesterone levels are normally higher (luteal phase). These higher levels of progesterone affect our breathing and, therefore, our outflow of carbon dioxide. After ovulation, and a few days beyond, carbon dioxide levels are at their lowest. When our carbon dioxide is lower, it contributes to our PMS problems.

Lower carbon dioxide levels are associated with the worst oxygenation of the body during our cycle. Carbon dioxide content is already lower, and due to that we begin stress breathing. If carbon dioxide content is already lower than normal due to ovulation, an increase in progesterone level can result in an even lower level of carbon dioxide! So . . . when we feel the best on days 1 through 14 of our menstrual cycle, it coincides with the **highest** level of carbon dioxide in our blood and the **lowest** level of progesterone. Basically, **breath** is directly correlated with our hormones, and therefore is intrinsically a part of unleashing our superpowers.

During the last week of our cycle, while carbon dioxide levels are plummeting and our progesterone is at its peak, impaired breathing can cause major issues within our hardware. Some of the biggest issues are stress and difficulties with concentration. Even though the brain and nervous system only make up 2% of our body weight, they use up to 20% of the oxygen that we consume. If our breathing is worsened, our body will take in less oxygen. Impaired breathing habits can play an important role in several problems that occur during our cycle.

The first one we want to talk about is stress, which also makes it difficult to concentrate. Our brain is the organ that suffers the most when we start to lack oxygen, and when oxygen is limited, we start working at a slower pace. A natural reaction from stress can be hyperventilation---or breathing quickly. The problem arises when stress is triggered and our breathing becomes faster than the body requires.

A lot of the stress that we experience in our day-to-day life isn't followed by any physical activity, so it's super common that our breathing equals a low-grade form of hyperventilation. Although! This isn't as bad an image as we stereotypically picture. But when this breathing pattern is repeated hour after hour and day after day, it can have a huge negative impact on our brains and their ability to make our human hardware function at peak performance.

The second thing that negatively impacts us when our breath is out of whack is asthma. It's been commonly known that asthma symptoms worsen before our bleeds and some studies have shown that 40% of cis-women with asthma are affected by "pre-menstrual asthma," or "a flaring up of asthma right before they bleed." As the results vary depending on a different setup of studies on the definition of asthma, more and more studies have shown that this is super common. Asthma is a condition that impairs one's ability to breathe due to a narrowing airway, limiting the airflow to our lungs.

There's a close connection between asthma and impaired breathing habits. And, as we discussed earlier, we as menstruating humans can have impaired habits because of our hormones. There was a survey conducted among women with asthma, inquiring as to the relationship between their asthmatic symptoms and their menstrual cycle. Of 57 women with asthma, 19 (or 33%) experienced a significant worsening of total pulmonary system scores during their pre-menstrual period---meaning the late luteal phase, the menstrual event, or both---with a maximum increase in wheezing and chest tightness during their luteal phase.

The third negative effect that breathing can have on our menstrual cycle is mood swings (sounding familiar?). When we're frightened or nervous or worried, we start to gasp for air. The frightened feeling when we're in the ER or visiting someone who is in trouble normally makes us gasp for air, tense up, and freeze---which is obviously the opposite of what we want for the mobility of our human and internal hardware. There is an old phrase, "Now that the dangers are over, we can relax and breathe out again." This phrase helps to illustrate that our breath freezes our hardware and makes it hard to unleash our superpowers.

Mood swings can be caused by any gamut of reasons, but when we get stressed or tense, we move our breath into our chest and it's like we're running from our fears. This reduces the movement of our diaphragm---which is our most important breathing muscle---and actually gives us the opportunity to grow past our discomfort. When a lack of diaphragmatic breathing happens in tandem with our low levels of carbon dioxide, we can feel like we are drowning in stormy waters, thus causing heavy mood swings.

In panic attacks and the fear of flying, it's common to breathe into a bag so a part of the air you breathe out is inhaled. Exhaled air contains a lot of carbon dioxide---100x more than the air we breathe in regularly---and when we breathe in our exhaled air, we naturally raise the carbon dioxide levels of our bodies. Therefore, a person in a state of distress can become calmer. It's almost as if carbon dioxide is our body's natural tranquilizer. In the work of Andrew Byrne, the author of *The Singing Athlete* (2020), he discusses the interconnection between the brain, breath, and our entire respiratory system. Our diaphragms, psoas muscles, and intercostal muscles have a daily exercise routine to keep us going---imagine what flexing those muscles looks like while harmonizing with our hormones, too.

The fourth negative effect that locked up breathing can have on our menstrual cycle is period pain and migraines! People like to generally root for oxygen, but we have to harp more on carbon dioxide here. Because carbon dioxide has a huge impact on our superpowers, it has a widening and relaxing effect on the smooth muscles found in our blood vessels, airways, stomach, intestines, uterus, etc.---basically our entire internal hardware. Impaired breathing results in that lower level of carbon dioxide and it contributes to the pain we may experience during our bleeds, which then causes cramping in the uterus. Carbon dioxide is a relaxing agent, and our uterus thanks us for it. This relationship means that we can enhance or reduce pain based on our breathing. If we tense up, our pain increases. If we find a way to relax, then we can decrease the pain and cramping.

During shallow breaths, we are overusing our accessory muscles in our chest, neck, and shoulders, rather than harnessing diaphragmatic breathing. Exhalation is usually a passive process where the breathing muscles are not active, but overuse causes the muscles to become tense and causes shoulder and neck tension. So, we basically breathe wrong all of the time. Since the chest is connected to our spine, the tension can spread into our back and cause back pain as well. The neck muscles also connect to our head, therefore gripping neck and chest muscles can cause headaches and even migraines! Essentially, if we trained our bodies to breathe correctly, many of our physical ailments would exhale out with the excess carbon dioxide.

The fifth issue that comes with impaired breathing is breathlessness. This means that breathing becomes worse to the point where it's *hard to breathe* and we start to feel breathless. Many menstruating humans complain specifically during their heightened progesterone time---the luteal phase---they feel breathless, especially if they do any kind of physical activity. It has a direct correlation with our hormones and breathing techniques.

Lastly, to come back to a holistic view, the sixth way that impaired breathing causes issues for menstruating humans is weight gain. We know it sounds pretty far-fetched that *air* can fluctuate our weight---but it can! Improving your breathing is simple and often overlooked, but can increase fat-burning and improve digestion, thus contributing to how much fat we carry in our bodies. In the conversion of nutrients to energy, the nutrients mainly consist of fat and sugar. Our body then requires oxygen to be readily available for that fat to be burned.

During ineffective breathing, less oxygen reaches the cells. And the worse our breathing is, the more we are closing the door to our fat reserves, in turn, causing digestive issues. Let's say that again . . . a lack of airflow causes digestive health failure and creates fat stores. When we don't have access to our fat reserves, we are forced to use ---or crave---a larger portion of carbohydrates than normal. When we overuse sugar as fuel, the relatively small amount of carbohydrates stored in our bodies as glycogen run out faster, and then we start to crave sugar to replenish them. (Check out our previous chapter for suggestions on how to crowd out sugar cravings.) Shallow breath doesn't give us the stimulation that low breath does for our stomach, liver, and intestines, and therefore it's harder for us to digest the food that we eat. In order to assist our digestive tract, our hardware is in desperate need of retraining our breath to include our diaphragm.

Bodies are complicated feats of engineering, and the control center---the brain---needs a lot to function at a high level. Our brains are selfish organs, and if we are lacking in overall oxygen, our brains will steal more, causing other organs and processes to fail in function. We then end up feeling terrible symptoms like menstrual cramps, since there isn't enough oxygen and carbon dioxide in our bodies to perform processes like shedding the lining of our uterus during our periods.

Now that we've talked about all of the things that can go out of whack due to *impaired* breathing, let's talk about ways that we can improve our breath so we can unleash our superpowers. Coach TL's eight favorite ways to improve breath and upgrade the connection to her cycle include:

Your Toolbox to Unleash Your Superpowers

1. Diaphragmatic Breathing and Massage
   i. This is the process in which we create awareness of the diaphragm muscles and separate the organs in the abdomen from the lungs. This type of breath is what professional singers practice to increase lung capacity.
   ii. (Massaging the diaphragm can loosen tension that builds up in your sides and around the uterus, while also improving bloating.) ---graphic below
2. Circle Breathing
   i. This is the process in which we take the same amount of time to inhale and exhale. If your natural rhythm is to inhale for 4, you also exhale for 4. (This isn't to be confused with Square breathing (in for 4, hold for 4, out for 4, hold for 4---a technique Coach TL recommends during the luteal phase to combat PMS symptoms.)
3. Posture Practice
   i. Since the lungs are soft structures, they only take up the room that you make for them. The best posture practice is to sit tall reaching your arms overhead, creating space for your lungs and engaging the diaphragm. Bonus Feature: this is great for gaining abdominal strength too!
4. Laughter!
   i. Some say "laughter is the best medicine". In this case, it is a great way to engage abdominal muscles/intercostal muscles in the breathing process, while also increasing lung capacity.
5. Hydration Station
   i. Getting enough water is HIGHLY important for the lungs (as well as the rest of the body). Fluids help keep the mucosal linings in the lungs thin, which helps the lungs function more efficiently.

6. Straw Breathing
    i. This technique is used in the vocal community in order to increase lung capacity. Andrew Byrne refers to it as our vocal push-ups. You place a straw between your lips and try to breathe in and out with the same amount of pressure. (If you do this inside of your water bottle you can observe the bubbles in the water upon exhale as a gauge for pressure).
7. Bellows Breathe (or breath in place of caffeine)
    i. This technique signals the body to be more alert and energized. Sit up tall and let your shoulders fall away from your ears. Keep your mouth closed and inhale/exhale rapidly through your nose, short quick breaths. Do this for 10-15 sec, take a break and try again. This is also called breath of fire---it creates a warming sensation within your human hardware.
8. Diamond Belly
    i. Find the space between your two hip bones, belly button, and pubic bone; we call this the diamond belly. This area is a part of our diaphragmatic breathing, but it is also where our pelvic floor is located. This technique requires a towel or yoga mat rolled up and then placed between your thighs and diamond belly. Hang your body over and then breathe deeply, the object causes resistance and strengthens/creates awareness for the pelvic floor.

Your Toolbox to Unleash Your Superpowers

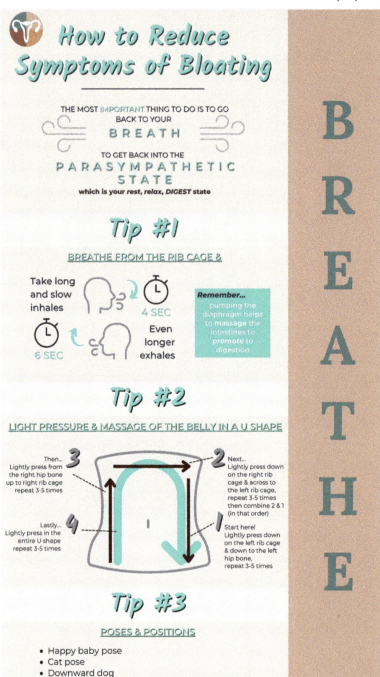

Breathe

place the rolled up towel between your thighs and diamond belly

Breathe into your pelvic floor

Feel your sits bones seperate and come back together

There are so many ways to improve breath work, but the most important is to hone in on the inner workings of your breath system in order to find harmony with your hormones and unleash your cyclical superpowers.

For a more in depth look at breath, check out the book Breathe: The New Science of a Lost Art *by James Nestor; it is very informative on breathing practices and breath transformation.*

TL;DR
BREATHE

- » Breath can be used as a form of medicine.
- » The hormone progesterone specifically affects breathing.
- » Lower carbon dioxide levels are associated with the worst oxygenation of the body during our cycle.
- » Breath is directly correlated with our hormones and therefore intrinsically a part of unleashing our superpowers.
- » Even though the brain and nervous system only make up 2% of our body weight, they use up to 20% of the oxygen that we consume.
- » There are many ways our breath can be impaired; but making breath work a practice can drastically improve your cycle and help unleash your superpowers.
- » 8 ways to make breath work, work for you:
  - ~Diaphragmatic Breathing and Massage
  - ~Circle Breathing
  - ~Posture Practice
  - ~Laughter!
  - ~Hydration Station
  - ~Straw Breathing
  - ~Bellows Breathe (breath in place of caffeine)
  - ~Diamond Belly

Your Toolbox to Unleash Your Superpowers

Chapter 8
Movement as Medicine

When we think of exercising or wiggling, we often think of strength and flexibility. However, with an infradian cycle specifically, we want to hone in on optimizing our mobility. So what does that mean? Mobility is the ability to move your human hardware without restriction, while hyper focusing on range of motion and injury prevention.

As our minds and bodies change throughout the cycle, our movement needs also vary---just like our food or fuel needs change as our hormones fluctuate. Interestingly, even during our "rest" phase, movement is a form of medicine. If this sounds confusing, don't worry! It's all part of finding that harmonious dance of our hormones and hardware.

As we begin the cycle and we are actively bleeding, reflection and rudimentary steps are necessary. Our menstruation phase is about reprocessing and reflection. Therefore, wiggles should include a review of our less rigorous movement patterns. This is a time to reinforce some of our skills gained in the previous cycle. Our human hardware is always looking for that fine balance between adaptability and stability. When we are actively bleeding, our movement focus should be geared toward balance and stability. Some of Coach TL's favorite go-to wiggles during this phase include an activated figure 4 and core-engaging dead bug.

 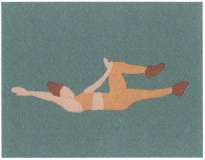

We know that when Aunt Flo comes to visit, you may want to just curl up in a ball and melt into the sheets. BUT we also know if you set yourself up for success the rest of the cycle, your energy will ebb and flow with the superpowers---making it easier to do the hard stuff, even when you're bleeding.

As we move into our follicular phase and the estrogen/energy levels kick up, we can use our movement medicine to channel superpowers, while also leaning into the adaptability of our hardware balance. During your follicular phase, it is good to get your wiggles on/going; our bodies actively seek bigger motion and interaction. With all this spring-like energy, now's the time to try something new. Maybe you've always wanted to learn to do a handstand; today's your lucky day! Your brain and body are the most receptive to new information in this phase, so it's the perfect time to learn a new physical skill. Coach TL's favorites include: BEAST crawls and squat variations.

Your Toolbox to Unleash Your Superpowers

Additionally you will feel the urge to increase the intensity of your wiggles, perhaps include cardio, and begin interacting with others. Challenges, classes, and sweat are welcome companions as we unleash the superpowers of your escalating estrogen.

AND THEN BAM! You're ovulating---this means follicular+++ (or follicular energy on steroids). You will feel ready to be in beast mode! The most exciting thing about ovulation is we are at a lower risk of injury. So this is the time to push yourself, take on risks, and FLIP THE DANG TIRE! This is our superhuman phase.

During this peak energy time, we are interested in group activities. Social environments are where we thrive, and we can ask the world for what we need/want. Our faces become more symmetrical, we give off 'give me what I want' pheromones, and we are at our peak 'learn a new wiggle' time. Coach TL's favorite wiggles for ovulation include Burpees and Throw the Ball Against the Wall (or even better, pass it to friends for more social interaction).

Lastly we enter our luteal phase. During this phase, we are in a sort of wind down/preparation time. Coach TL calls this phase the taskmaster phase. Now is the time for circuit-based wiggles---our brains are checking items off the list and then doing them over again; we need less variability during this time. We feel the need to be more methodical and to review things, rather than try new ones. Move from cardio to resistance-based movement, reduce the intensity of your movement routine, and notice that you are able to read others. This ability makes you tactical and ready for competitive sports. Some suggestions from Coach TL include CARs and Bow and Arrow.

This type of movement is hyper focused on range of motion and the methodical management of joint health.

As you move through your cycle (both physically and figuratively) it is important to take note of where you are. These are all guidelines of how wiggles can improve your day to day journey as a menstruating human, but knowing what your hardware is asking for is a process of getting to know your body through trial and error.

So often, society shows us we are just "tiny men." The textbooks for most certified physical trainers (CPT) have an asterisk at the bottom of a page on how to train "women" (menstruating humans); but we know differently, and it is important that we integrate our cycles into all parts of our routine. As a menstruating human, you have more essential fat, carry most of your lean mass in your lower body, and have a greater proportion of slow twitch muscle fibers* than that of cis-men. Also, you're naturally good fat-burners---which is great for endurance, but can cause a need for a boost when you need to access stored carbs to 'go hard'. These are all facts about our physiology and they are facts that can help us to train for our cyclical nature, rather than as an asterisk (or tiny man).

*Slow twitch muscle fibers, or endurance type I fibers (aerobic), are present in all bodies, as are Fast Twitch Muscle fibers, or power type II fibers (anaerobic). The difference is: Menstruating humans tend to be laregly comprised of Type I endurance fibers while cis-men are comprised mostly of Type II power fibers.

TL;DR:
MOVEMENT AS MEDICINE

- » You are not a tiny man---so don't train like it!
- » Menstruation Wiggles are about reprocessing and reflection; we are entering a less rigorous routine.
- » Follicular Wiggles are about ramping up, trying something new, and challenging yourself.
- » Ovulatory Wiggles are full on BEAST MODE! Flip the tire, get social, take the risk.
- » Luteal Wiggles are taskmaster moments. This is the time to prepare, be methodical, check off the list.
- » Every set of human hardware is different. Check in with your body and learn what it is asking for.
- » The most important measurement of all is the answer to, "How does my human hardware feel today?"

Your Toolbox to Unleash Your Superpowers

Chapter 9
Mental Gymnastics

"...it's the end goal of every patriarchal culture. Because a very effective way to control women is to convince women to control themselves."
--Glennon Doyle, Untamed

For our purposes, menstruating humans are taught to live a life where bleeding is normal but practically unmentionable. We are conditioned to "control" the flow of big feelings that come and go in order to fit the societal norm. We hold such innate power, but the whole bloody mess must stay tucked away in case we offend or make folks uncomfortable. So we keep it a secret.

This cultural pit of shame is set to ensnare you with as simple a comment as, "what, are you on your period?"---said with the same indignance as if you passed gas into a microphone during a sermon. Periods are treated as if we had the choice, as if we become dirty. And our feelings,

... those are to be kept in check at all costs. The only thing more offensive than period blood is BIG FEELINGS! So we downplay our feelings, bleed in secret, and invest so much precious time in hiding. Imagine what we could accomplish if we invested that energy elsewhere? We develop code names and elaborate ways to discuss our "dirty little secret"; we tell folks it's 'shark week' or that 'aunt flo' came to visit. We discreetly slip products to one another in order to shield the world from our honest experience as a menstruating human. The word *period* wasn't even said on television until 1985 in a tampon ad by Courtney Cox (Peach 2020). And that shame drain is exhausting. Shame takes us down a path of feeling less than; our periods and feelings are something to push through, and therefore we end up spending HALF our life (on average we will bleed between 600-700 times) wishing it was over. . . . That is practically the definition of wishing your life away.

Brene' Brown defines shame as the "intensely painful feeling or experience of believing that we are flawed and therefore unworthy of love and belonging" (2015, 69). Our culture has endless solutions available designed to convince us that we need fixing and improving, without actually giving us any resources to understand ourselves at a basic level; most menstruating humans will grow up knowing more about the cycle of the washing machine than they know about their OWN cycle. We don't know what we aren't taught, and shame prevents any open dialog---causing suffering in silence---which breeds shame, and then the cycle continues. A survey, conducted in the UK, of young menstruating humans showed

- » 48% of those surveyed are embarrassed by their cycle;
- » 79% of them have concerns about symptoms such as heavy bleeding, irregularity, and severe pain;

» 54% said they hadn't sought medical assistance because they thought their symptoms were normal; and
» 27% said they were too embarrassed to speak with a medical professional.

(This is partly why conditions such as endometriosis, discussed in Chapter 11, are under-diagnosed and folks suffer excruciating pain but are too embarrassed to ask for help.)

We are here to encourage you and empower you to exit the hall of shame and unleash your superpowers. Part of that journey starts by reflecting on yourself, and never apologizing for your period. Returning to the idea of what goes up, must come down; what if that isn't a pessimistic outlook after all? What if it is exhilarating, like a roller coaster or jumping on a trampoline for the first time? What if there is just as much richness in the descent as there is in the rise? Our mental health in relation to the powers of the period is vital in order to reach our peak performance.

Fun Fact:
Speaking of peak performance, what better proof of embracing the inner superpowers and implementing our cycle than the US women's soccer team leading up to the World Cup? "USWNT coaches for the first time in the team's World Cup history tracked players' menstrual cycles and symptoms and instituted practices to help players perform their best" (Kindelan 2019) was the headline. Coach Dawn Scott, high performance coach for both the USWNT and the National Women's Soccer League, credited the breakthrough of period tracking as one of the strategies the team "deployed that helped us win" (as cited in Kindelan 2019). Each player's training schedule was bespoke to her cycle, working in sync with her human hardware---telling her when to work for more gain, when to catch more zz's,

and what foods were going to support her in each phase. The US women's soccer team is already a talented group of individuals---add in the superpowers of their internal human hardware and . . . MAGIC!

Speaking of magic, have you ever taken a moment to sit in awe of your body and the CRAZY number of complex processes it goes through every day without you even thinking about it? Our hormones, brain, and gut work together to carry us through the world as a high functioning being---we should be thanking it, not judging it . . . especially if it's giving us Big Feelings.

We know these feelings can be hard to explain or understand, so let's delve a little deeper. What are we being told when we are so very weepy, or hot-headed suddenly, and why does it seem like we don't have control? These feelings are our hormones speaking to us through each part of our cycle. We are feeling the depths of our intuition we discussed in Chapter 2; we are surging with energy and passion during our ovulation event. This big wave of emotion is a physical and emotional manifestation of our hormones giving us direction. We can harness these signals and utilize the big feelings for a productive and colorful life.

The best news about BIG FEELINGS is we can channel them and use them to face the darkest parts of ourselves with humility, grace, and courage. All that coal also hides diamonds in the rough. These gems are our biggest teachers and greatest treasures. The more we discover about this part of us, the better equipped we are to face any challenge. If we instead suppress these feelings, we miss our mine of diamonds---because containing the hardest parts also contains the beauty. Power lies within channeling our feelings---being, doing, giving and taking---when the time is right. Superpowers in practice. As Abby Wambach says in her book *Wolfpack*, "New Rule: Be grateful for what you have AND demand what you deserve" (2019, 25).

TL;DR:
MENTAL GYMNASTICS

» Patriarchal shaming cages menstruating humans, keeping us ignorant to our own innate superpowers.
» Leaning into our cycles can be a fast-track ticket to peak performance--just ask the US Women's Soccer team on how they won the world cup!
» Holding space for our BIG FEELINGS can help us turn coal into a mine of diamonds.
» Our bodies work with magic every second of our day---forget body shaming, let's be grateful and bask in awe!
» "New Rule: Be grateful for what you have and demand what you deserve." ---Abby Wambach

Your Toolbox to Unleash Your Superpowers

Chapter 10
Birth Control and Hormonal Replacement Therapy

Now that we've covered all of the groundwork of how our bodies can function and thrive under ideal hormonal conditions, let's get into the opposite end of the hormonal spectrum. We're talking hormonal birth control (not the hormone-free copper IUD) and HRT (hormone replacement therapy).

According to the CDC, roughly 24% of menstruating humans utilize some form of contraception, with a little over half of that using the oral pill. And roughly 0.4% of the US population has used or is using HRT to affirm their trans journey. If you fall into any of these categories, you probably wrestled with whether or not this book could help you; maybe you even skipped ahead to this chapter hoping for a quick answer.

The quick answer is that there is no quick answer. For our purposes, we consider a menstruating human to be anyone who has the propensity to plan for a period or pregnancy if they stopped taking certain medications or treatments---but how hormone-controlling treatment affects your unique biology is something that only you can answer with your lived experience.

What do we mean by that? Well, let's get into some visuals! A menstruating human with balanced hormones and cycling freely can feel a gentle ebb and flow to their hormone superpowers. They experience peaks and valleys and, with each crest or dip in the wave, their brain chemistry and human hardware is shifting into a different gear.

Some people cycle freely but *don't* have balanced hormones. Whether they have PCOS, PMS, or even the stress-inducing PMDD, their hormones don't feel like a gentle wave; they feel like a deadly roller coaster. Their brain chemistry and human hardware aren't merely shifting gears, but are instead making fast, erratic, and harsh changes throughout their different phases. Their infradian rhythm can feel like this.

Whereas for folks on hormone controllers, their infradian rhythm can feel anywhere from barely audible to completely muted. For example, if you're on hormone blockers or take the combination pill (of estrogen and progestin, a synthetic progesterone), then the bell-curve of studies say you most likely fall into the "completely muted" category. *But* there are so many different kinds of hormone controllers out there, both in HRT and contraceptives, and they each are perceived by the body in different ways. Not only are the options for hormone controllers all different, but as we've been saying all along, menstruating humans are very different from each other.

Our variance is one of the reasons we are so under-researched. The bell curve used to determine results in medical studies is a lot less clear-cut when your biology is programmed to menstruate. So, while some folks on hormone controllers might go about their days feeling completely unchanged from week to week and day to day (what we would call the "completely muted" infradian rhythm), some folks may notice a slight difference in their energy levels, brain chemistry, and human hardware from week to week. Their infradian rhythm is quietly meandering along, being corralled into nearly a straight line by the hormone controllers, but still providing some semblance of difference throughout their month-ish. For these folks, their infradian rhythm can feel like this.

To folks working with HRT, this might not be a surprise, but to the folks working with hormonal contraceptives, this might be brand new information: as living beings, our hormones affect our brain chemistry. So when we take compounds to change our hormones, we are *still* changing our brain chemistry.

Hormones are our human hardware's boundless messengers, delivering directions and data to and from sources all throughout our tissues. For this reason, it's impossible for hormones to be "localized." Our hormones don't even stop at our skin---our "hardware's barrier."

Your Toolbox to Unleash Your Superpowers

Remember how one of our superpowers during ovulation is being able to turn heads just by walking in a room? A part of that is because of *pheromones*, which are hormones our bodies give off as a means to communicate with receptive individuals in our environment. When we take hormone controllers, we are doing more than just controlling our menstrual cycle: we are altering a highly complex and streamlined system that functions as a regulator for jobs as extraneous as attracting a mate through pheromones to as crucial as operating our brain chemistry.

Most of the research on how hormone controllers affect our brain chemistry comes from studies done on the combination pill. But, fun fact, the progestin in that combination pill is made from testosterone, and our bodies will perceive it as such. That altered testosterone can have so many negative effects on our human hardware (for some people; again, *we are all different*), that newer *generations* of the combination pill contain testosterone blockers to keep the progestin from binding to testosterone receptors and running amok in our endocrine pathways.

This means that even our *natural* testosterone can get blocked from doing its job, leading to low libido, liver problems, low blood count, depression, weight gain, cardiovascular disease, hot flashes, breast soreness, and all kinds of other issues (Bergen 2021; Osborne 2018); but Coach Korra is getting sidetracked. Sarah Hill, author of the book *This is Your Brain on Birth Control* (2019), likens hormonal contraceptives to running through a house, randomly turning light switches and electronics on and off. She also alludes to the fact that one day we might realize the method to the seemingly randomized madness, but we have barely scratched the surface with our understanding of how the combination pill affects our human hardware (Hill 2019).

We don't say this to try and scare people off from working with their hormone controller of choice. HRT is vital to the health of some trans folks, and hormonal contraceptives have been an equally vital key to women's social progress. We say this to continue to deliver the message that *you know your body better than anyone*. Better than us, better than your doctor, even better than the entire scientific community!

So, if you came to this chapter looking for the quick answer to "how does your hormone controller affect your superpowers," the quickest answer we can give you is that *only you can know*.

With that in mind, let's take a look at some loose knowledge on different hormone controllers and how you might be able to find where you are in your cycle if you do feel that your infradian rhythm is hovering around "barely audible."

THE BARELY AUDIBLE INFRADIAN RHYTHM

Before we delve into how you might be able to find where you are in your cycle when you're on hormone controllers, we have to provide the disclaimer that this method that Coach Korra and Coach TL use has virtually no Western modern science to back it up. Instead, it's based on what Coach Korra likes to call "ancient wisdom." If you take issue with that, that's fine. Until the medical community begins to include us in the research to the degree that we need to be included, we've found that using older practices to fill in some gaps can help menstruating humans navigate their personal journeys with less guess-and-check and more direction.

Long ago, when human beings were still evolving---back when the discovery of fire was blowing everyone's minds, and maybe even before then---human beings lived in small communities. Life expectancy wasn't all that high, so roughly half of the community was comprised of menstruating humans---which is a lot of period tracking to keep up with.

There's a prevailing myth that "we all sync up to each other," which isn't completely accurate. We could cite a study done on a Chinese dorm building full of menstruating humans to prove that we don't all sync up to each other, but that study didn't take into account one very important factor: **light**. For probably our entire existence, human beings have maintained biological schedules that revolved around light. Our circadian rhythms follow sunlight, even if you don't rise and fall as the sun does. Whether you are what sleep biohacking source Dr. Michael Brues calls a *lion* (traditional "morning person") or a *wolf* (traditional "night owl"), your sleep and daily biological circadian rhythm still revolve around when the sun goes up and when the sun comes down.

Menstruating humans, unlike circadian-only folks, don't rely only on the sun's light, however. Our month-ish long cycle tends to respond to the light from the moon, too.

For those who don't know, the moon has a 28-day long cycle---which, suspiciously, is the median length for balanced menstrual cycles. The moon's month-ish starts at the *new moon*, where the moon is dark and provides no light, and waxes until it becomes a *full moon* about two weeks later. Anyone who has seen a full moon without light pollution can attest to how bright a full moon is. On super full moons, when the moon is close to the earth, it can even completely lighten a landscape. Then, for the next two weeks, the moon's light wanes until it is completely dark--- completing the cycle and existing as a new moon once again.

To reiterate, the moon has an *event*, with two weeks of ramping up energy into the culmination of another *event*, to wind down and repeat the process all over again. Sound familiar?

Your Toolbox to Unleash Your Superpowers

If you don't get a period, either because you're on birth control, HRT, or just simply don't know where it disappears to every month, there is a method developed from ancient wisdom that talks about how menstruating humans cycle with the moon!

It turns out we don't sync to each other, we sync to light.

Folks who are focused on themselves: students, busy workerbees, folks digging into inner child work, folks relishing in self-care, etc. tend to get their period on the new moon and ovulate around the full moon

Period-Free Flow Key

Folks who are focused on nurturing or growing something outside of themselves: parents, business owners, gardeners/farmers, folks taking care of family members, etc. tend to get their period on the full moon and ovulate around the new moon.

Folks without a period/on outside hormones don't ovulate, and without ovulation the depths of our superpowers are... well made less deep. Think kiddie pool compared to the deep end

But if this is you, your body may still be ever-so-subtly cycling and might continue to until you reach menopause.

For this reason, we recommend using the moon to track where you may be in your cycle.

The kiddie pool isn't the deep section, but you're still in the water, and that's what we're here to help you with!

*For more information like this, check out The Superpowers Planner!

Birth Control and Hormonal Replacement Therapy

Following this technique from ancient wisdom, we can find that, in general, menstruating humans with balanced cycles will be on one of two types of cycles: those that get their period on the new moon and ovulate on the full moon, and vice versa.

Ok, you might be thinking, but then how would one know which cycle they're on if they don't get a period?

The general rule of thumb is to look at where your energy is directed. If you are tending to something outside of yourself (a business, a garden, children, animals, the elderly, etc.) then you are most likely on the cycle that would bleed on the full moon and ovulate on the new moon. Older sources call this the *mother cycle* or the *red moon cycle*, but we like to refer to it as the *nurture-focused cycle*. The flip side to the nurture-focused cycle is what we like to call the *self-focused cycle*---you can still be *nurturing* yourself, but you might be vibing with this cycle if your energy tends to be more self-focused. This cycle tends to present in students, artists honing a craft, and people who are focused on a journey of self-care and self-love. The self-focused cycle bleeds on the new moon and ovulates on the full moon.

The best theory we've heard (and like) about how this might have developed was that it created a division of labor and care within our early human communities. On the new moon, a large chunk of the group would be bouncing around in high-energy ovulation; they could pick up the slack from another chunk of the community who would get their bleed at the same time, who were primed instead for downtime and reveling in juicy intuition. It also created less competition between menstruating humans for baby-making matches. And then two weeks later, the previously bleeding menstruating humans would ovulate and take care of the menstruating humans who had taken care of them on their bleeds. We like to think of it as a built-in mechanism that demonstrates just how human beings evolved to take care of each other, and to ensure that we could thrive with community care.

Something important to note, however, is that while our bodies may have developed this technique to respond to light at night, we no longer live in a world where the only lights at night are from the moon and stars. If you're like Coach Korra, and you've never seen the full night's sky because of city light pollution, it's very possible for your cycle, with or without hormone controllers, to be "off" from what you'd expect. This also goes for folks who are in transition from one energy focus to the other, like fresh graduates starting a new business, or parents with aging children who are discovering they have more time again to take care of their own needs.

When Coach Korra addressed this on her social media, there was a massive outpouring of excitement from viewers looking at the lunar calendar for the first time and realizing that this was holding true for them! And we think it's really exciting, too. No matter how removed we think we are from nature and the environment that we evolved in, there are still things that tie us to the most fundamental parts of life on earth.

For any of our menstruating humans on hormone controllers, clueless about how or where to even begin to understand their cycle, we recommend checking in with a lunar calendar and your energy (are you feeling outwardly nurturing most days, or more self-focused?), and see if you're feeling a little more sluggish and intuitive (indicating your period superpowers are trying to come through) or more social and interactive (indicating your ovulation superpowers are trying to come through).

Something else we think is important to address about this moon-cycling technique is that it is merely a tool. It is not a determinant of your worth, value, or some ethereal grandiosity. If using the moon to track where you might be in your cycle helps you connect to your glorious human hardware better, *amazing*. If it doesn't, that's cool too! That then becomes data for what doesn't work for you---which, in the long run, is still really helpful to know.

Speaking of data, we need to address the data that *is* out there about what current science knows about hormone controllers and how they might affect us and our human hardware.

EFFECTS BIRTH CONTROLS HAVE ON OUR HUMAN HARDWARE

As we mentioned before, there are many different types of hormonal birth control on the market, and they affect us all differently. The form that has been researched the most is the combination pill, which contains both estrogen and a synthetic form of progesterone, called progestin. Where an unhampered menstrual cycle resets every month-ish, folks who take a daily pill are resetting the same day of their cycle over and over again. Which day? Well, with the combination pill the day is somewhere in the luteal phase. The combination pill works, essentially, by telling our brains that we are in the post-ovulation phase so that ovulation is completely removed from our brain's hormonal to-do list.

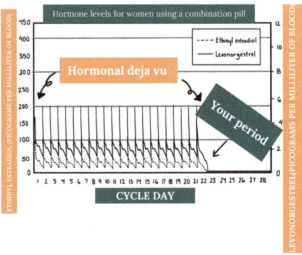

Before you thumb back through the book to remind yourself of the ins and outs of the luteal phase, we have to add that the pill isn't *only* making your brain think it's in the luteal phase---in fact, it is doing far more.

The luteal phase's superpowers are characterized by winding-down energy, an endurance for tackling tasks and long to-do lists, nesting, a heightened metabolism, decreased oxygenation, and a heightened stress response to stressful triggers.

Let's start with the unsavory element of the luteal phase, the heightened stress response. As you may recall from Chapter 9, cortisol is the main hormone running the show when our human hardware needs to feel stress to a certain trigger. The cortisol, while it may seem like our ultimate enemy, is actually incredibly useful for keeping us afloat and alive in environments that could otherwise put us into shock and have us unhelpfully unresponsive.

Most folks cycling freely feel extra stressed by triggers when they're in their luteal phase, and the research is showing that folks who take the combination pill, which tricks the brain into resetting the same day of the luteal phase over and over again, will still report feeling just as stressed as someone off the pill, *but they don't have the cortisol surge to back it up.* The combination pill completely disrupts the body's hormonal stress response to triggers, meaning that while folks might *feel* stressed in their brain, there are no signals going out to the rest of their body to react to the trigger, or to protect the tissues and organs from the stress. This is something humans tend to only experience when they are burnt-out or undergoing massive chronic stress.

What the research is telling us right now suggests exactly that: the combination pill overwhelms a person's nervous and endocrine system to the point where their human hardware can no longer react to triggers of stress. And because cortisol is the hormone we rely on to get us up in the morning, there is evidence that the combination pill can not only mess with the menstrual cycle, but a person's circadian cycle as well.

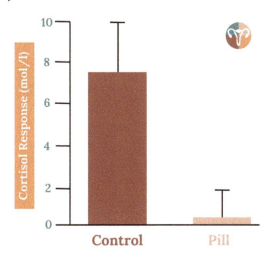

Yikes! You might be thinking, *why would anyone go on the pill then? This sounds terrible!* Well, not all menstruating humans are the same---we are all very, very different from each other. For some folks, these out-of-whack stress systems and cycles don't feel so bad. Some folks might even find that they're an asset for certain chapters of their lives. The story of the pill isn't the same for everyone, and there's a lot more we can say about the combination pill. But we're only going to address one more major aspect of the pill that makes it different from a regular day in the luteal phase, and it's something we've mentioned before: the fact that our hardware thinks the synthetic progestin is also testosterone.

During our luteal phase, testosterone levels are low. In fact, the only time testosterone increases is during our ovulation event; it's a part of what makes us feel confident and horny. But the combination pill messes with our hardware's perception of testosterone, which can mess with the luteal phase superpowers we might have otherwise gotten. It also has been shown to have overall "masculinizing effects on the brain, doing things like decreasing verbal fluency and increasing performance on mental rotation tasks" (Hill 2019, 85). Which, again, for some folks works just fine with where they are in their lives, while for other folks, this is the least helpful list of side effects they could hope to receive.

Luckily, there are four different generations of the combination pill and each upgraded generation works to address a different issue with our hardware's confusion on how to read progestin. The newest generation even goes as far as to include anti-androgens that bind to testosterone receptors in the body to block any progestin from acting as testosterone. The negative---or positive---bonus feature here is that the anti-androgens also block naturally occurring testosterone from doing their job. The generation of combination pill a person is taking can completely change their experience because, again, not only are there multiple forms of contraception out there (both hormonal and non-hormonal), but every single menstruating human will react differently to what they're prescribed. If you're on the combination pill and you haven't been enjoying your experience, talk to your doctor---and if they aren't open to talking to you about it, get a new one!

When we control our hormones we can control our brains---to an extent. We might not all be able to hold onto our hardware's innate superpowers when we take different hormonal contraceptives and controllers, but then again, some people might *want that*. Birth control has been vital in bringing menstruating humans the level of financial and professional development we have reached today. Is it for everyone? Heck no! Is it a good tool for some folks in different stages of their lives? Heck yes!

OK, sure, you might be thinking, *that's great for folks on the pill, but I'm not on the pill. So how does my hormonal contraceptive affect me?*

The other forms of hormonal birth control are way less researched than the combination pill, and even if they weren't, your best data point is always going to be you.

HOW TO TURN YOUR EXPERIENCE INTO DATA

Step 1: Acquire a space to write in---a journal, the notes app on your phone, a blank word document, etc.

Step 2: Write down your energetic, physical, emotional, and mental experiences of the day. Try to keep a consistent rubric going so it's easy to compare days. On a scale from 1-10 how was your brain fog, energy, libido, sleep, appetite, etc.

Step 3: Keep tabs on any factors that remain fairly consistent---these might be from your contraceptives.

Step 4: Bring them to your doctor. If they're not symptoms you want to keep living with, ask them about contraceptive alternatives that might be aligned with what you and your doctor know about your biology.

It is far easier to see how your contraception is affecting you when you use this system before and after starting it. You can also be solidified and informed even further if you talk to a friend or family member about your new experiment with hormonal contraceptives so they can give you an outside view of how it might be changing your brain. But even if you're already on hormonal contraceptives, there is no time like the present to start recording your experience!

Coach Korra is obsessed with fun facts, so we're going to list a few fun facts about hormonal birth control here:

» Smell plays an important role in attraction. Many menstruating humans who were on hormonal contraceptives when they met their partners, and then went off of them, discovered that they suddenly

hated their partner's natural scent, or vice versa (went from disliking their partern's scent while on contraceptives to finding their scent maddeningly sexy when they went off contraceptives).
- » We are generally more attracted to people who have different immune systems than our own---to make for a healthier baby. Research done on menstruating humans on hormonal contraceptives found that they were more likely to be interested in partners with similar immune systems (Asprey 2020b). And one study done on children with food allergies found that more than half of the children's mothers were on hormonal contraceptives when they met their fathers (Asprey 2020a).
- » Hormonal contraceptives have been found to nullify our ability to pick up virility cues from potential partners. Straight cis-women on hormonal contraceptives were found to detect no difference when looking at faces deemed more masculine and when looking at faces deemed to be less masculine. Whereas freely cycling straight cis-women had a high attraction response to the more masculine faces during their follicular and ovulation stages.
- » Some users of the pill have reported that their pill experience had them no longer listening to or caring about music. When they went off the pill they found themselves signing up for Spotify and adding music back into their everyday lives.
- » There is a direct correlation between when birth control was made available to unmarried folks and when menstruating humans began outpacing cis-men in college and jobs that required higher degrees. One attribution is to the fact that we didn't have any accidental pregnancies. Another is to the fact that, for the first time in our entire evolution, we could *plan when* and *if* we would have children. That

allowed for menstruating humans to go all out in reaching for more demanding educational and career pursuits because contraceptives gave us reproductive autonomy.

    Our hope for you, dear reader, and our discussion on birth control, is that you take your healthcare into your own hands and that you *question* something as biologically altering as birth control---especially if your doctor doles it out with little explanation as to the effects it might have on your precious human hardware. You're allowed to ask questions; you're allowed to try different forms. The point being that it is your choice.

    And now that we've fleshed out some of the key points to birth control, it's time to dive into another form of hormone controller, the types of hormone controllers genderqueer folks use to affirm the experience they want and need to have with their human hardware.

HRT & A NOTE FROM OUR CONTRIBUTORS

    Many folks in the queer community that are transitioning take hormones, but not all; it's a personal decision. Not all people who menstruate are women---this is why we use the term "menstruating humans." Periods can be inconvenient or superpower-filled no matter your gender. But if you are trans or non-binary, they can be a source of gender dysphoria. Talking about your body and experience can sometimes be the best way to combat dysphoria. We sat down with a couple of folks to chat about their experiences with HRT and cycles in order to highlight an underserved community that we know can benefit from their personal superpowers.

    We asked for stories about their periods and testosterone, and every reply was different. The varying effects of testosterone on one's cycle are huge, but---as with many aspects of trans health and menstrual health---this is something that remains under-researched.

US: HOW DOES TAKING TESTOSTERONE AFFECT YOUR CYCLE?

"Before taking testosterone, my period was light and regular, though easily interrupted by physical stress like over-exercising or anxiety. I had some PMS and cramps, but they were pretty minor. After starting testosterone my period stopped originally, then returned once (a single, "normal" cycle) when I switched from Sustanon to Reandron." ---Jesse

"My period immediately stopped after my first injection and I haven't had a period since. CRAZY!" ---Tobey

"I started my period at 12 years old and started HRT at 22 years old. After about 124 cycles I didn't have to deal with the horrific symptoms that plagued me throughout high school. I always had bad headaches and horrible cramps. When I started HRT, my estrogen levels were already low, so the doctor just had to up my T. I was excited when my voice dropped from an alto range to a tenor because I can finally sing songs I loved and couldn't before. About 6-12 months after I started T I stopped feeling most emotions. I became super apathetic aside from really low mental health days and obvious stuff like laughing at a joke or excitement re: my niece. I still struggle to reconnect with feeling and acknowledging emotions in general. My emotional life doesn't seem to have the same range. One of the most anxiety filled experiences was using the men's bathroom while still having to use period products. Although I do remember a time I was opening up a tampon and a guy in the other stall said, 'Man . . . you got a bag of chips in there? Must be a long one . . .' and I got a good chuckle out of that. I definitely had an uptick in sex drive after starting T." ---Mitch

"I started taking T in 2016. One month after I started I had my final period, and it was the period from HELL! I was cramping and in pain---it made me feel sorry for those folks who dealt with those symptoms regularly. I initially started my period when I was 14 y/o and it was one of the most lonely times in life. I didn't talk about it with my parents because they were not interested in talking about it; it was almost shameful. I had to ask my big sister. For all of high school, my cycle was so irregular; I had a lot of anxiety around it because I never knew when it was coming. The best part of taking T is I almost immediately felt like a superhero . . . the first time I carried all the groceries in alone I was ecstatic." ---Jayme

US: DO YOU FEEL ANY OF THE BENEFITS OF YOUR CYCLE NOW THAT YOUR HORMONE LEVELS HAVE CHANGED AND YOU DON'T NECESSARILY BLEED EVERY MONTH?

"Before I started testosterone, I had extremely bad cramps and my period lasted 6-7 days each time. I had a really heavy flow and an irregular cycle. After taking T for some time, I have noticed a shorter length in my period. It has gradually become less heavy and more irregular. I am thankful for no cramps, and I feel the benefits of a heightened sex drive." ---Andrew

"I think I feel the fluctuation of appetite you would from the cycle, but I also noticed that since I started HRT, I never get full the same way. I know when to stop eating, but never have that after-Thanksgiving overly-full moment. For me, the best relief was having top surgery. I know it isn't to do with the uterus, but once I had it done, I felt like it had taken away a negative that was producing anxiety." ---Mitch

"I resonate with the cyclical nature of the monthly cycle still, especially while in a relationship with a menstruating human. I feel the intuition benefits, but it is harder to cry now. It can stress me out when I want to show empathy, but I have a harder time showing emotion. I also miss the energy boost estrogen gave to go work out RIGHT NOW! When I first started T, I had some sad moments because I didn't feel music the same way; it wasn't as deep. I used to be really moved by music---like I could almost drown in it---but once I started T the music wasn't as colorful. I was also worried about losing my female singing voice, but I am happy with my lower voice now, and I feel more even keel. I think losing my period was a plus." ---Jayme

No matter what your journey is, being able to talk about it with others is important. If you or someone you know needs help finding a trans-friendly healthcare provider you can visit **wpath.org** or check out our resources listed at the end of the book.

OUR JOURNEYS

Both of us, Coach Korra and Coach TL, are prime examples of how different hormones can affect different bodies differently. Coach Korra discovered quickly that her body does not like taking hormone controllers, and Coach TL has found superpower bliss with a hormone implant. We're not kidding when we say everyone is different!

Coach Korra's birth control experience was short-lived, and for good reason. Having a history of depression, Coach Korra was prescribed the low-ogestrel pill, a daily oral contraceptive that wasn't even designed to be a method of birth control. The number of hormones in the low-ogestrel pill is roughly one-third the dosage contained in the average oral contraceptive, as it was designed to help menstruating humans with postpartum issues to transition out of pregnancy. Immediately her body rebelled. Her doctor prescribed it because it had the lowest chance of aggravating her mental illness. Unfortunately, it had the opposite effect.

"At that point in my life, I had always been on the heavier side, but the pill I was on made me gain even more water weight---but at the same time food didn't taste so amazing. I'd never had a problem with acne, but all of a sudden, I had big breakouts every bleed. The mood swings were awful, and my depression, which used to be fairly manageable, was absolutely crippling. Every month, when it came time for the sugar pills it was like I was sinking deeper and deeper into an accumulative numbness. I started skipping the sugar pills just because I didn't want the fog to get worse. Thankfully, I was seeing a health coach at the time who explained to me that in skipping the sugar pills I was doing more harm than good by essentially digging myself a deeper hole.

"The brain fog was so terrible that when I broke not one, but *two* blood pressure machines at a checkup, and the nurse was trying to hide her panic because my blood pressure was so dangerously high, it didn't compute to me. I went 'oh, that's weird,' and left without connecting literally any dots. It wasn't until I went off of the pill and the fog started to lift that I realized the way the pill was affecting my blood pressure could have potentially killed me. It took almost two years for all of my terrible symptoms to go away---some of which I hadn't even realized I was experiencing. The reason I went off of it was because it made my depression debilitating, but once I went off of it I realized I had saved myself from so many other destructive side effects.

"The weirdest part of the whole experience was when I saw my doctor a few weeks after going off of it she, one, tried to pin my lingering, still-high blood pressure on my weight and the lifestyle she assumed I lived because of my weight (AKA: fat-shaming me), and two, tried to coerce me into trying a different hormonal contraceptive to replace the one I'd kicked. I understand they're all different and can have different effects, but at that point I was just starting to feel like the world had some color again. There was no way I was going to experiment with something that could throw me back into the listlessness. My mental, physical, and emotional health are too important."

We'd like to add to Coach Korra's story, that if your doctor shames you, doesn't listen to your concerns, or tries to coerce you into a treatment you aren't comfortable with, get a new doctor. They are not gatekeepers on your health journey, they are advisors and guiding partners who should be open to working *with* you to find out the treatments and practices that are most beneficial to the life you want to live. For Coach Korra that means cycling freely. She is very fond of condoms and the app Natural Cycles---the only app whose algorithm has a patent with the FDA as a form of family planning---to keep her aware of where she is in her cycle, as well as in charge of when she gets to start her (future) family.

Coach TL, however, has had quite a different experience with hormonal contraceptives. Having started her period at a later age than most the girls around her (15), she felt like she was behind the curve in knowing how to deal with the sudden change. Although she had strong women in her life, the shame drain discussed in Chapter 9 was strong with her. Coach TL grew up in dance and was an exceedingly active, young person---now, with this new obstacle, she felt dirty and less capable. Every time her period came, she dreaded going to dance, partnering, or even thinking about dawning her leotard. It didn't help that there was NEVER any warning.

"My cycle was incredibly irregular to start. I would bleed for 10 days (EXTREMELY HEAVY) and then not have a period again for months. I was in a constant state of worry that it would come at the 'wrong' time. When it did arrive, I agonized over how I thought I smelled, and I also dreaded having the conversation with my mom that liners weren't doing the job (the flow was too heavy), but pads were like diapers on me. I felt so much shame I asked my older sister to teach me how to use a tampon and had her purchase them for me. This constant worry and stress lasted all through high school. When I finally arrived in college, I found that creating my own schedule, choosing my food, and finding time to relax helped regulate my cycle. I also noticed that during tech week (I was a performance major) or finals week, my stressors spiked and therefore I felt a crazy surge of hormones and then my periods would be extra wonky. When I went to my first pap-smear, I discussed with the doctor ways to help with my irregularity."

So often we use birth control as hormonal control---but this isn't best for everyone. Looking back now, Coach TL can see that doctors easily go for that option, not thinking about the dampening of the superpowers we can access. The conversation went something like, "If you are wanting more control of your cycle, we should discuss birth control options. We have many ways to regulate when you get your period and how heavy it is . . . these are your options . . . blah blah blah." The pill sounded awful---one more thing to keep up with, major side effects such as depression, acne, and bloating . . . no thanks! And Coach TL was entirely too nervous to get the copper IUD---even though it was the non-hormonal option---because her dear friend had it and scared her out of it with the horror of the pain after insertion. (TL is an enneagram 7 and has a DEEP fear of physical and emotional pain). After much consideration, the Nexplanon implant is what she decided would work for her.

"My doctor and I discussed all the side effects and possible outcomes. One of the most appealing things initially (since I had little to no knowledge of the rest of my cycle) was that I could likely not see my period all year! When I first got the implant that is exactly what happened. I didn't get a period for 9 months, then I got a NEVER-ENDING period. It went on for a month. I was worried so I returned to my doctor. She said that it wasn't out of the norm, and if it was too annoying, she could prescribe a pill to help. I was annoyed that I was now looking at having two different hormonal changes. I declined and decided to do some research. Now this was very early on in my journey toward the discovery of our SUPERPOWERS, so give me some slack, but I found a couple articles on behavior changes to help 'go with the flow'. Once I implemented these small changes, I began to feel like I knew exactly when I was going to bleed."

  Coach Korra came into Coach TL's life not long after and the rest is history. Their unlikely meeting sent the little bit of research and wonder spinning into action. They met over 75 cycles ago and every cycle for coach TL has improved, feeling more of the depths of the power we carry in us. Birth Control is certainly not for everyone, but it does regulate the flow of Coach TL's uterine lining, and she lives with much less shame and doubt around the bloody brilliance her uterus can provide.

TL;DR
BIRTH CONTROL AND HORMONAL REPLACEMENT THERAPY

» There is no short answer to how your infradian rhythm is affected by hormonal contraceptives and HRT. Only you can say how it's affecting you!
  ~A balanced cycle has a wave of gentle ebbs and flows.
  ~Some people on hormonal contraceptives and HRT can experience a muted wiggle/wave to their infradian rhythm.
  ~And some people experience their infradian rhythm as an erratic roller coaster.
» Folks taking hormone controllers that make them skip periods may be able to follow the moon's cycles to discover where they are in their cycle.
» The most researched form of contraceptive, the combination pill
  ~confuses our body and runs around acting like testosterone---or blocks all testosterone, even our own naturally occurring;
  ~resets our cycle so we are living the same hormonal day of the luteal phase over and over again; and
  ~stresses out our brains to the point where our nervous system cannot react to stressful triggers. This makes for burn out and a perpetual state of shock.
» Losing your period from taking T does not mean you can't reap the benefits of your internal physiology.
» Body dysphoria is real, and being able to talk about it is one of the tools we suggest in order to cope.
» Everyone reacts differently to different hormone controllers: what's important is how *you* feel.

Chapter 11
Imbalanced Hormones and Health Conditions

Our superpowers are the product of a delicate dance of different hormones coursing through our hardware, requiring a completely different mixture of hormones per phase and event, each measured out to create the perfect balance month after month.

Sounds like a lot of work to maintain, right? Well, you'd be correct in that concern. The good news is that most of us are able to maintain something close to this balance just by the pure might of our biology; when our human hardware is under strain, the bodily function that suffers *isn't* always our reproductive system.

According to more holistic health sciences---and the writer of *The Autoimmune Fix* Tom O'Bryan (2016)---we all have a "weak link" in our biology, either from our genetics or our environment. We all have something that's generally the first to give when we aren't able to maintain "perfect health." For some folks, it's their digestive system, others their nervous system, others their ability to focus or sleep.

But now, after finally laying down the foundation of how our bodies can operate in ideal scenarios, it's time to address those months and those folks that don't automatically bathe in a perfect reproductive hormone balance; it's really common to experience either.

For some people, this is their weak link. For others, it's a big red flag on top of a series of other red flags. And most commonly, it's just someone's bad month. Either way you experience it, let's talk about the ways our cycles can go wrong.

SMALL IMBALANCES

You don't need to have a serious condition to experience a rough menstrual month-ish. Due to the nature of the infradian rhythm---lasting several weeks before it begins again---there is far more data and factors being taken into account at its every turn than our daily circadian rhythm. This inevitably means that each of us are bound to experience a rough cycle at one point or another during the course of our long chapter as menstruating humans. For the most part, these intermittent, or barely consistent, and problematic cycles don't mean that you are in need of instant medical prevention, or that there is something super wrong with your human hardware. It can be as simple as what we like to call a *slight hormonal imbalance.*

These are the main types of slight imbalances that any one of us may experience:

TOO LITTLE ESTROGEN

Too little estrogen is a common culprit for elongated cycles. Folks who can easily go six or even twelve weeks between periods may find that their cycles become more regular, and shorter, when they give their hardware the support it needs to up its estrogen levels. Remember, our cycle's length revolves around when we ovulate, and the estrogen peak in the middle of our cycle is what signals ovulation to occur. So if it takes someone four weeks to build up the amount of estrogen that a balanced cycle would build up in two, they are bound to have a longer cycle.

Too little estrogen also can show up as having long, light bleeds and some terrible PMS before your bleed because your estrogen levels are not balanced with the progesterone during your luteal phase.

According to Alisa Vitti (2019), having too little estrogen can be seen in your period by having a light pink flow. We have yet to find any evidence of Alisa Vitti's "Flow Types" outside of her work (and she doesn't share her sources), so please take this technique with a hefty grain of salt.

It's worth noting this isn't the only cause of elongated cycles. This is a possible cause that you can remedy yourself at home*, but if this doesn't work, or you suspect this doesn't apply to you, working with your health practitioner is your best bet to get to the root of the problem.

How does one balance too little estrogen? Engage with naturally occuring phytoestrogens like soybeans, tempeh, and natto (natural, fermented versions of soybeans), flax seeds, sesame seeds, oats, barely, yams, mung beans, pomegranates, licorice root, mint, ginseng, fennel, anise, red clover and spinach. Avoid hormone disruptors like BPAs and the stuff found coating paper receipts. Engage with sugar and caffeine less (both will take precedence over reproductive hormone build up and break down), and prioritize sleep and activities that bring you joy!

*See home remedies in Chapters 6 and 8.

TOO MUCH ESTROGEN

Too much estrogen has rather heavy symptoms. The biggest sign that you might have too much estrogen cycling through your human hardware will appear during ovulation.

Starting out one's cycle with too much estrogen will lead to an excessive amount of estrogen halfway through one's cycle when estrogen production is designed to peak. The most common symptoms are acne and anxiety during one's ovulation. Fatigue during ovulation can also be a sign of too much estrogen. And if someone's liver hasn't broken down the excess estrogen, then too much estrogen can be seen by PMS---specifically with mood swings and fatigue that don't stop until one's period is over, or even until ovulation is over---and can also be seen by heavy bleeds. Having too much estrogen can be seen in your period by having a purple or chunky flow (Vitti 2019).

    If you suspect you might have too much estrogen, the name of the self-care game is liver support. Avoid as many phytoestrogens and hormone disruptors as you can (see the list above in "*Too Little Estrogen*") to get strict with your self-care game during your luteal phase when your body is already sending out directions to break down estrogen. Engaging with different liver supportive herbs, like dandelion leaf and milk thistle, can also be a huge help---especially if you find it hard to put down the coffee, sugar, or alcohol, all of which distract your liver from doing the work of breaking down the extra estrogen.

If these symptoms sound like what you experience regularly, but you have even more symptoms, please keep reading and bring what you learn to your health practitioner. Some of the more serious and chronic conditions have symptoms that overlap with having too much estrogen.

TOO LITTLE PROGESTERONE

    In Coach Korra's health coaching practice, too little progesterone was the most common hormone imbalance she saw in folks who found their cycles to be, at worst, a mild nuisance. Progesterone is a key player in the luteal phase, but doesn't do much outside of that, so folks who have too little progesterone may commonly find that their cycles are totally fine---right up until their last week of their luteal phase.

Unlike estrogen imbalances, which are created from the signals of our human hardware, in our luteal phase, progesterone is made from the *corpus luteum*---the ex-home of the unfertilized egg from that cycle's ovulation. The corpus luteum is what creates the progesterone for our luteal phase. Because progesterone is a precursor to cortisol, it's very easy for our bodies to use too much of that progesterone during cortisol production, leaving our luteal phase with too little progesterone.

The luteal phase is ideally characterized by the inwardly-focused superpowers, but when we have too little progesterone, we lose those superpowers and are instead given poor sleep, a heavy appetite, and very high stress levels. Similar to having too much estrogen, folks may find the most help from focusing on liver and stress support during their luteal phase with an extra emphasis on eating more complex carbohydrates to mitigate the body's stress response so it produces less cortisol. According to WomanCode by Alisa Vitti (2013, 154), having too little progesterone can be seen in your period by having a brown flow (but once again we haven't seen these sources).

PCOS

Polycystic Ovarian Syndrome, or PCOS, is a complicated hormone disorder with a wide range of symptoms and subtypes. Symptoms can range from extreme physical symptoms like consistent weight gain, excess body hair, chronic fatigue, irregular periods, and cystic acne to feeling completely fine and having a totally unremarkable period; except the person's PCOS is completely blocking their ability to conceive. PCOS can be blatantly obvious or super subtle. Roughly 15% of menstruating humans have PCOS, and of those, 70% don't realize they have it. As well, there are multiple types of PCOS a person can experience. And because a person can be diagnosed with a combination of subtypes, it's a tricky hormonal disorder to pin down.

The most common form of PCOS is insulin-resistant PCOS---that's insulin resistance for the entire cycle, not just during the already insulin-resistant luteal phase.

Inflammatory PCOS generally comes with elevated testosterone levels and a messed-up ovulation event.

Non-traditional PCOS type 1 is characterized by insulin resistance and messed-up ovulation events without the elevated testosterone of inflammatory PCOS.

And non-traditional PCOS type 2 is characterized by insulin resistance and elevated testosterone, but with a healthy and issue-free ovulation event.

Approximately 30% of folks who have PCOS don't have the namesake, polycystic ovaries. And just because someone has cystic ovaries doesn't automatically mean they have PCOS. Generally, two out of three factors need to be experienced:

» Polycystic ovaries,
» Irregular cycle and period lengths, or
» Elevated androgen hormones, like testosterone.

And, lastly, this isn't a criterion for a diagnosis but is a common enough symptom that we have to mention it: current studies show that about 80% of folks with some form of PCOS are considered medically obese*.

*Please note that medical grades given to body weight are inherently racist and sexist. We are only including this symptom to help folks follow the thread to any potential, unseen hormone unhappiness. Having a human hardware that can fall into the medically obese category is not an automatic judgment on your worth or even your health.

Some health practitioners will dole out hormonal birth control as a person's only means to mask whatever symptoms they're experiencing, but it's important to know that, while this form of treatment has the potential to make PCOS symptoms go away, it does not fix the underlying issue (a Band-Aid over the check engine light moment). When folks go off the hormonal contraceptives, whatever form of PCOS they experienced is right there waiting for them on the other side. Oftentimes, the condition and its symptoms are worsened because the person's human hardware wasn't given the resources to straighten out whatever was going wrong in the first place. But, ask Alisa Vitti of FLO Living (who put her own PCOS into remission) or any of the wonderful doctors at the women's health clinic Tia, and you'll find that a more holistic approach to treating PCOS requires a multi-pronged approach; a combo platter, if you will.

Depending on what type of PCOS a person has, any combo of blood sugar, liver, stress, anti-inflammatory, metabolism, and even emotional/psychological support or therapies may be necessary. Some functional doctors, like the ones who work through the company Tia, will prescribe acupuncture treatments for their PCOS patients on top of other therapies and supplements. But it can take a long time to get both a diagnosis and a doctor who has your back, and you shouldn't have to wait---especially because most of the work for managing PCOS happens outside of a doctor's office anyway. So let's go over a few methods that we use with our own clients.

Taking the cue from Alisa Vitti, getting enough micronutrients is crucial for PCOS support. Coach Korra's favorite solution for anyone struggling to get enough micronutrients is to drink a quart of deeply brewed nettle tea every day. Her favorite herbalists at Commonwealth Herbs like to say that nettle tea is so micronutrient dense, that "if you don't feel like eating a vegetable that day, just have some nettle tea!" Now, neither Coach Korra nor Coach TL would advocate for skipping out on veggies, but it shows just how nourishing nettle tea is. Other teas that are especially helpful are teas that reduce inflammation or regulate blood sugar like burdock, green tea, chamomile, and turmeric tea.

Additionally, a lack of Vitamin D and E can exacerbate PCOS pain, so tackling that deficiency can be especially helpful. Foods like tuna, nuts, broccoli, pasture-raised egg yolks, and sunflower seeds are all high in Vitamins D and E. But we can also get Vitamin D from sunlight, and while the amount of sunlight that's healthy for your skin will vary depending on your local UV index, the generic rule of thumb is that 30 minutes of morning sunlight is generally safe for Vitamin D levels and hormone regulation.

It's important to note that we need the nutrient magnesium in order to absorb Vitamin D and receive its pain-dampening effects. We can bake in the sun all the livelong day, but if we're deficient in magnesium, we won't absorb enough of it. Good sources of magnesium are foods that we talked about in Chapter 6; foods like goji berries, chocolate, spinach, and pasture-raised eggs. But if you're in the market for a supplement, magnesium citrate is a good supplement to start with because if you take it before bed it'll help you fall asleep too! This will also help with PCOS problems because sleep is important for hormone regulation!

Coach TL always asks clients how much water they are drinking, no matter the situation. This is especially important with PCOS since water intake flushes sodium (which causes inflammation) from the system. The other piece to the combo platter is the specific wiggles that can alleviate pain or discomfort; the most useful is pelvic floor breathing (mentioned in Chapter 8). This technique releases tension and cramps while connecting us more deeply to our human hardware. Just remember, while navigating PCOS there is no one size fits all solution.

Some health practitioners find a lot of success from working with supplements, food, exercise, and lifestyle factors as a means of regulating the unhappy hormones wreaking havoc in PCOS; some practitioners, like Alisa Vitti of FLO Living, even see patients' PCOS go into remission. If this route intrigues you, we've included some well-known PCOS helpers in our resources section. As well, it's important to know that hardly any of these more holistic methods work instantly---whereas an aligned contraceptive can nix symptoms in as little as a few days. However, the holistic methods have the ability to nix not only the symptoms, but also the cause, thereby saving someone from worse PCOS down the line.

However you may choose to navigate your PCOS journey is your own decision to make. PCOS is not currently a curable condition, but it is a condition that can be mitigated and even put into remission when we are given the support and tools we need to sort through the mess and thrive in our everyday lives.

ENDOMETRIOSIS

Endometriosis is a condition where a person's uterine lining grows outside of their uterus. One case even reported a woman whose endometriosis was causing her uterine lining to grow on her vocal cords. The condition can be anywhere from blindingly painful to completely painless, and the only way to know for sure that someone has it is to find the endometriosis tissue, wherever it is growing in a person's hardware. Because of this simplistic method for diagnosis, it's one of the most misdiagnosed conditions menstruating humans experience.

For those who do experience pain from endometriosis, there seems to be a common threat from spikes in their symptoms because the tissue causing the pain (and inflammation) is triggered to grow from estrogen. As such, these folks may experience up to three weeks of symptom flare-ups every cycle---their safest time of the month-ish being just before and just after their periods when their estrogen levels are low. Whether or not these folks have a happy period or a wretched period seems to be a toss-up, as the pain they experience throughout their month affects the report card presented via their menstrual events.

Coach Korra has advised a few folks to see a doctor about getting an endometriosis diagnosis, and something she noticed was that a common symptom was shooting pains up and down the legs several times a month, consistently at the same time every month. If you have any inkling that you may have endometriosis, we implore you to talk to your healthcare practitioner about it.

In conventional Western medicine, hormonal contraception is normally the first treatment to tackle endometriosis. But, much like with PCOS, the contraceptives don't change the fact that there is an underlying condition upsetting the person's hardware; they only mask the symptoms. For some folks, this is all they need and want, but for others---especially for those who want to conceive, or simply don't do well with hormonal contraceptives---this first option of treatment is not the answer they're looking for.

There are a range of surgeries one can undergo to remove or nullify the offending tissues. If this is a route you or anyone you may know wants to go down, we have to stress the advice that you go to a specialist who has successfully performed the surgery before and, above all, listens to you. There are one too many horror stories of menstruating humans who received a botched endometriosis surgery, or a type of surgery that turned out to be the wrong surgery for their condition, and it made their symptoms worse. In the US, finding a doctor who specializes in endometriosis is difficult, but we have found a small directory of doctors who can help folks wanting to see a doctor for treatment. (See our resources section at the back of the book for this list.)

The last thing we'll mention about endometriosis is that holistic practitioners have reported having a lot of success with their endometriosis clients by focusing on food lifestyle, specifically an anti-inflammatory diet. Much like with PCOS, this route of treatment doesn't cure the condition, but it can put it into remission. We have included a list of health practitioners that specialize in helping folks down this road of endometriosis in our resources section as well.

PMDD

The last big condition we're going to address is a grumpy little condition called premenstrual dysphoric disorder, or PMDD. Unlike PCOS (which tends to center in the ovaries and cause clear physical and emotional distress) and endometriosis (which can live literally anywhere in our human hardware and tends to cause physical pain), PMDD is theorized to be centered in our brain and is mainly known for causing disturbances in energy levels, mood, and cognition. And if you recall from our talk about food, because our brains and guts are so intricately connected, PMDD can also come with a lot of disruptions in our bowels.

PMDD is a relatively new discovery to the Western medical community (we say that ironically as menstruating humans have been experiencing it far longer than the medical community has acknowledged it for), and so far it is thought to be "an abnormal reaction to normal hormone changes that happen with each menstrual cycle" ("Premenstrual..." n.d.).

It's considered to be an exacerbated form of PMS---a symptom of an unsupported menstrual cycle---but to talk to folks who experience PMDD, it is far more debilitating than PMS. Some folks with PMDD will have only one clear-headed week out of their entire month, while others find that their symptoms are downright crippling, but maybe only during their luteal phase. Either way, it is a very serious condition and not one that can be cured by "powering through"---so let's remove that burden from your shoulders.

Your Toolbox to Unleash Your Superpowers

Because PMDD is so new to Western medicine, no one has a surefire fix for it. However, experts from alternative therapies have gotten some patients results by working with the same tools we've been harping on throughout this book: movement, stress management, nutrient-rich foods, sleep, and taking care of yourself. Especially because PMDD tends to have such a heavy effect on the gut-brain axis, working with things that improve your microbiome (food, wiggles, sleep, and joy) are all tools that can help you tame the PMDD monster.

However, we understand that fatigue and brain fog can be two of the biggest hurdles PMDD bestows on those who suffer from it, and therefore the idea of "taking on" a toolbox to fend off PMDD symptoms can feel like a catch-22. Let us suggest a first step for you if you think you might suffer from PMDD: ask for help.

Tell your parents, your partner, your therapist, your roommate---anyone who's consistently in your life who can offer a hand of support on the days when PMDD seems like it's taken away your ability to cope and function. Sometimes, having a lighter load to carry on our hard days can make all the difference in our ability to carry that load. And from there, things can snowball *for the better.* Ultimately, we want every menstruating human who suffers from PMDD to have an orchestration of support tools ready to go on any given bad day of their cycle, but that takes time. We're superhuman, but no one can build Rome in a day.

If you suspect that your cycle may be butting heads with PMDD, we advise you to seek support. Talk to your health practitioner. Seeking out alternative forms of healing like acupuncture, health coaching, and herbalism can be beneficial substitutes or supplements to working with the treatment a doctor may provide. Because PMDD is still so under-researched, it's completely fair to feel frustrated at how under-equipped our society's conventional routes to

Imbalanced Hormones and Health Conditions

treating health problems are for whatever you're experiencing. But it's important to remember that PMDD *is* not something you have to power through.

Our parting word of advice regarding PMDD is this: just because it's a reaction seemingly centered in our brains, doesn't mean that it's "all in our heads." PMDD is a very real and very serious condition that no one should be belittled for or gaslit into ignoring. There is a podcast about PMDD aptly named "Power Over PMDD" (Sairs 2020) because PMDD is a condition we can get the better of. We just need to give ourselves the time and patience to develop our own superhuman plan of attack.

TL;DR:
IMBALANCED HORMONES

- » There are three types of slight hormone imbalances:
  - ~Too little estrogen
    - categorized by rough periods, elongated cycles, and late ovulations
  - ~Too much estrogen
    - categorized by anxious and acne-ridden ovulations and heavy periods
  - ~Too little progesterone
    - categorized by high-stress luteal phases, exhausted periods, and PMS the days leading up to your period
- » Polycystic Ovarian Syndrome, or "PCOS" is a hormone disorder that is difficult to diagnose because it has multiple types and symptom sets.
- » So far, the most success in treating PCOS is found in working with food and lifestyle tools. Using a mix of these tools can even put PCOS into remission!
- » Endometriosis is a serious condition where the uterine lining grows outside of the uterus--and it can happen anywhere in the body! The most helpful treatments to nix the pain include:
  - ~hormonal contraceptives,
  - ~Surgery, and
  - ~anti-inflammatory diets.
- » Pre-Menstrual Dysphoric Disorder, or "PMDD," is a disorder where the reproductive cycle's hormones have an adverse reaction to a person's brain chemistry.
- » PMDD has a strong tie to the gut-brain axis, so working with food can prove immensely helpful.
- » But overall, reaching out for support to make your burden lighter is the best first step!

Chapter 12
Now Go Out and Live Your Superpowered Life

You've got the power---now it's yours to get out there and get down to it! You don't have to go out there and shout about your period to everyone, unless that makes you feel the most empowered. Just imagine living your daily life with the agency to actually feel to the fullest and chat about your body; imagine if people asked and actually listened. However you decide to go about unleashing your superpowers, doing so cultivates pride and is an act of love. Love for yourself.

You now have the tools to experience your month to its fullest. BE, DO, GIVE, TAKE. Each change of your multifaceted self is a precious resource to be tasted, tested, and held as a triumph. Weekly change that provides us four ways to move through and see the world. Four ways to channel our desires and feelings in order to create the change we seek to make.

We're talking WAP WAP WAP that's...

Why Apologize for Period?

As a menstruating human, you've got a lot going on.

Start your powerful self revolution.

Biohack your cycle.

Unleash Your Superpowers.

Recipes
For the different phases of your cycle

These are only one example for each phase of the cycle. For more recipes like these, keep your eyes peeled for our seasonal cookbook coming out soon!

Curated by Chef Julia deGruchy

UNLEASH YOUR SUPERPOWERS

FOLLICULAR FOOD
CHERRY BASIL SMOOTHIE

Ingredients:
- Juice 2 limes
- 3-4 fresh basil leaves
- 1/2 cup of plain coconut yogurt
- 1 scoop of vanilla protein powder
- 1 frozen banana
- 1/2 cup of frozen cherries

Blend, Top with crunch, Enjoy

UNLEASH YOUR SUPERPOWERS

OVULATION FOOD
PECAN CRUSTED SALMON

Ingredients:

- 1lb of salmon filets, skin on is fine.
- 1 cup of crushed pecans
- 1/4 cup of corn starch
- 3 Tablespoons of salt
- 1 Tablespoon each: chili powder
- black pepper, garlic powder,
- onion powder, & dried parsley.
- 1 Tablespoon of butter
- 1/2 a celeriac root (celery root)

- 2 cups of spinach
- 1 cup of dried apricots
- 1/4 cup of lemon juice
- 1/4 cup of apple cider vinegar + 1T
- 1 teaspoon each: turmeric, chili powder & salt
- 1 Tablespoon of a neutral oil

UNLEASH YOUR S♀PERPOWERS

OVULATION FOOD
PEACAN CRUSTED SALMON

Instructions:

1. Apricot Coulis: In a small saucepan add 1 teaspoon of salt, 1 cup of water, 1/4 cup ACV & dried apricots. Cover with a lid and bring to a boil for 5-7 minutes. Without opening the lid, turn down the heat to a simmer for another 5 minutes. This is rehydrating the apricots, they should be plump once you open the lid, and only a bit of liquid should remain. Cool for 5 min then put all of the pots' contents into a blender with the lemon juice, spices, 1T ACV and oil. Blend till shiny & silky smooth.

2. Wilted vegetables: Use a very sharp knife to slice off the bumpy ends of the celery root. Peel off the layer of rough skin. Celery root is naturally off-white with some discoloring. Cut it in half, save the 2nd half. Use your vegetable peeler to shave the root into long strips; start on the flattest side. Try to get the most complete strips you can. Take your spinach and put the leaves on top of each other in little piles, slice each pile into 1in strips. Put all veg in a bowl and massage 1T of salt into the mixture. Let sit for at least 10 minutes.

OVULATION FOOD
PEACAN CRUSTED SALMON

Instructions:

3. Turn oven on to 400. In a medium bowl whisk the pecans, corn starch, 2T of salt & dried spices. Coat your salmon portions lightly in oil with either a paper towel or back of a spoon. Put a heavy bottom pan (cast iron/non-stick) on high heat. Dredge your salmon in the dry mixture, press gently to adhere the mixture to the salmon. Add 1T of butter to your pan, lay the salmon in the butter and turn the heat to medium. 2 minutes per side, baste the top of the salmon in butter before flipping. Put in the oven for 5 minutes.

4. Plate and Enjoy!

UNLEASH YOUR SPERPOWERS

LUTEAL FOOD
BRAISED BEEF & SQUASH

Ingredients:

- 1lb of beef stew cubes
- 2 teaspoons of salt & pepper
- 3 teaspoons of chili powder
- 4 teaspoons of cinnamon
- 4 table spoons of neutral oil
- 1 diced medium yellow onion
- 2 tablespoons of mined garlic
- 2 tablespoons of minced ginger
- 1/3 cup of cider vinegar
- 1 16oz can of crushed tomatoes
- 1 tablespoon each: coriander & turmeric
- 3 bay leaves
- 2 cups of diced butternut squash
- 1/2 cup of plain yogurt
- 2 cups of chopped spinach

UNLEASH YOUR S♀PERPOWERS

LUTEAL FOOD
BRAISED BEEF & SQUASH

Instructions:

1. Put the beef cubes into a bowl & toss with salt, pepper, 1tspn cinnamon & 1tspn chili powder.

2. Put a large skillet pan over high heat, add 3 Tbspns of oil, or just enough to coat the bottom of the pan. Add the onion, minced garlic & ginger. Let it start to brown on the bottom before you stir. Stir for another minute, then push the mixture to the edges of the pan, add a drop more oil, adding the beef to the cleared center of the pan. Let the beef brown on the bottom, about 2 minutes, then stir with everything else & turn the heat down to medium.

3. Deglaze the pan with 1/3 cup of white wine or apple cider vinegar. Add the entire can of tomatoes, coriander, turmeric, bay leaves & 1/4 cup of water. Cover & let simmer on mid-low heat for 10 minutes, then check beef.

4. While that's cooking, dice your squash. Butternut squash can be replaced with delicata or acorn squash. Put a medium pan over medium heat; add 1 tablespoon of oil & the squash. Let the squash soften & brown, stirring occasionally. Add 1/4 cup of water to the pan & cover quickly; continue cooking for 3-6 minutes, or until squash is fork tender. Uncover, sprinkle with garam masala & drop in the spinach, letting it wilt as you stir. Then dollop on the coconut cream or yogurt. Continue stirring with a spatula to incorporate it fully. It might "melt" a little, that's ok. If you want it less runny let it sit longer on low heat. Add salt & pepper to taste.

5. Once both are done, pile it up in a bowl & enjoy!

UNLEASH YOUR SUPERPOWERS

MENSTRUAL FOOD
MUSHROOM BURGER

Ingredients:

- 1-8oz package of button mushrooms
- 1 medium onion
- 2 tablespoons of minced garlic
- 1 cup of cooked & cooled brown rice
- 3 tablespoons of salt
- 1/4 cup of oats

- 1/2 cup of walnuts
- 1 tablespoon of corn starch
- 1 tablespoon chili powder
- 1 tablespoon black pepper
- 1 tablespoon paprika
- 3 tablespoons of a neutral oil

MENSTRUAL FOOD
MUSHROOM BURGER

Ingredients Continued:

Slaw
- 2 cups thinly slice purple cabbage
- 3 teaspoons salt
- 1 tablespoon honey
- 2 teaspoons sriracha
- 1 teaspoon paprika
- 1 tablespoon minced cilantro
- 2 Tablespoons rice wine vinegar or
- apple cider vinegar

MENSTRUAL FOOD
MUSHROOM BURGER

Instructions:

1. Wash & slice all your mushrooms & put them in a medium bowl. Small dice a medium onion; add to the bowl.

2. In a skillet, that has been fully heated over medium high heat, add just enough oil to cover the bottom of the pan; about 3 tablespoons. Add your sliced mushrooms & onion to the skillet along with the minced garlic. Let it cook for 2 minutes, stirring occasionally before turning the heat down to medium. Let cook until the mushrooms are soft and the onions translucent. Let this cool while doing the next step.

Recipes

MENSTRUAL FOOD

MUSHROOM BURGER

Instructions Continued...

3. In a food processor, add your 1/4 cup of oats & 1/2 cup walnuts; blend until they become a finer powder. Add the cooked & cooled brown rice, making sure not to add any stray liquid. (Extra liquid will make the burgers too soggy!) Add the corn starch, salt & seasonings; pulse blend to combine. Add the mushrooms from the skillet & continue to blend on high until a fluffy paste forms. Feel free to add flax seeds if you want! Heat your oven to 450.

4. Put the sliced purple cabbage in a small mixing bowl with the vinegar & salt, stir throughly with a fork. Add the honey, sriracha, paprika & cilantro; keep stirring.

5. There is the likelihood, depending on difference in cooking styles, that your mushroom paste will be a bit more wet & sticky than you'd like, & that's ok! Simply pan fry the burgers in a skillet with spray oil before putting them in the oven. Create your patties by using a shallow circular lid as a mold, or forming them with your hands. Bake on a parchment lined sheet tray for 20-25 minutes. Serve with the slaw on top!

UNLEASH YOUR SUPERPOWERS

The Infradian Rhythm
Superpowers + Support Cheat Sheet

Follicular Phase
Day 6-14

Superpower: Creativity, High energy, brain+ body retain new techniques + info like a child prodigy, heightened immune system, heightened nutrient absorption, adroit at problem solving

SUPPORT
Food: healthy fats, slow-burning grains, fermented foods, citrus, sprouts and micro-greens, leafy greens

Movement: HIIT, cardio, high energy and constantly changing

Mind: Plan your month, find solutions to the problems that came up in your last bleed, map out ideas and throw throw them against the wall to see what sticks!

Ovulation
Day 15-17

Superpower: Follicular+, adept in social situations, easier orgasms, speaking bears a happiness reward, perceived as more/very attractive to anyone who would be interested, risks are less risky.

SUPPORT
Food: Follicular+, nutrient-dense greens, bitter greens, better able to process alcohol + caffeine.

Movement: Classes, bring a friend, +literally anything (less likely to be injured, go for gold)

Mind: Ask the world for the impossible, you're more likely to get it (ask for a raise, go on a date, deliver your thesis, the list goes on!)

Weak Immune system starts here in Luteal

Luteal Phase
Day 18-28

Superpower: Stamina, Admin work

SUPPORT
Food: Complex carbs (root veggies and squashes especially), dark meat.

Movement: Check in with your body and move accordingly. Pushing in workouts ~1 week before your period will bring physical pushback

Mind: Boring tasks and duties may feel fulfilling and rewarding. Now's the time to stick with it and keep up the hard/good work. The stuff you threw against the wall in follicular, does it stick?

Part 1: ~a few days after ovulation
Riding the estrogen wave of ovulation, live in the best of both worlds

Part 2: ~a week before your period
Wind down and focus on internal themes. Stress management is key here. Nourish yourself

Part 3: ~3 days before your period
Just testosterone. Hit the weights!

Menstrual Phase
Day 1-5

Superpower: Intuition

SUPPORT
Food: Sea vegetables, magnesium rich foods (spinach, goji berries etc), non-fish seafood (clams, lobster, octopi, etc)

Movement: Restorative OR hit the weights

Mind: What feelings are coming up for you right now? Do you feel unsupported in your relationship? Ignored at work? Like you aren't enforcing your boundaries? Listen to those feelings. There is a difference between anxiety and intuition, and now is when intuition is a literal superpower.

@unleashyoursuperpowers

Cheat Sheet

UNLEASH YOUR SUPERPOWERS

Resources & Rad Products

Books

Fix Your Period by Nicole Jardim
Roar by Stacy Sims, PHD
This is your Brain on Birth Control by Sarah E. Hill, PHD
Period Repair Manual by Lara Briden, ND
Becoming Cliterate by Laurie Mintz, PHD
Come As You Are by Emily Nagoski, PHD
Doing Harm by Maya Dunesbury
Women, Madness, and Medicine by Denise Russell
Period Power by Maisie Hill
Beyond the Pill by Dr. Jolene Brighten
WomanCode & In the FLO by Alissa Vitti
The Body is Not an Apology by Sonya Renée Taylor
Policing The Womb by Michele Goodwin
Eat Like a Fish by Bren Smith
The Dental Diet by Dr. Steven Lin
The Autoimmune Fix by Tom O'Bryan, DC, CNN, DACBN
Breathe: The New Science of a Lost Art by James Nestor
The Singing Athlete: Brain Based Training for Your Voice by Andrew Byrne
Untamed by Glennon Doyle
Wolfpack by Abby Wombach

UNLEASH YOUR SUPERPOWERS

Resources & Rad Products

Apps

Tia
Natural Cycles
Moody
Feelmo
MyNormative
FitrWoman

Podcasts

Power over PMDD
Period Power
The Period Party
The Holistic Herbalism Podcast
I Weigh with Jameela Jamil
Body of Wonder

UNLEASH YOUR S🦪PERPOWERS

Resources & Rad Products

Products

Vagina pH friendly condom brands:

sustain
Sir Richard's
Lovability Condoms
L. Condoms

Sustainable Period Products:

DivaCup
Flex
Intimina
Knix (leakproof underwear)

UNLEASH YOUR S♀PERPOWERS

Resources & Rad Products

Finding Help

Resources for eating disorders:

www.betterhelp.com
https://lauraschoenfeldrd.com/
https://nourishedwithfarahalvin.com/
http://www.sonyareneetaylor.com/
http://www.colleenreichmann.com/

Specialists for Endometriosis:

https://www.endo-resolved.com/endometriosis_specialist.html
https://www.thisendolife.com/
https://endometriosisdietitian.ca/
https://thepelvicexpert.com/
https://www.katepowe.com/
https://beyondendo.com/

UNLEASH YOUR SUPERPOWERS

Thank You

We know now we are filled with superpowers individually---therefore together we can achieve greatness. We are beyond grateful for our amazing Superpowers Team. Gabi has seamlessly kept the brand beautiful and word spread wide. Madeline designed our groovy logo. Anastasia conjured up humor and joy in our marketing copy. Nataly designed the planner we hope you'll get to pair with this book. Katie labored over this book's every syllable and made our words legible and flow throughout this journey. Jinjer conjured and created the magical map you see, as well as our gorgeous cover art. Megan has kept Coach TL's head on straight. And together we make up a superpowered team of menstruating humans reaching out to boost others all around us. Thank you! You have all brought such joy to a difficult time in the world. Keep shining bright, and sharing your wonderful gifts.

UNLEASH YOUR SUPERPOWERS

Follow Us!

For more information about Unleashing Your Superpowers

Website:
www.unleash-your-superpowers.com

Instagram:
@unleashyoursuperpowers

Email:
hello@unleash-your-superpowers.com

Abd El-Lateef, Sayed M, El-Sayed M El-Sayed, Ahmed M Mansour, and Salama A Salama. 2019. "The Protective Role of Estrogen and It Receptors in Gentamicin-Induced Acute Kidney Injury in Rats." Life sciences. U.S. National Library of Medicine. https://pubmed.ncbi.nlm.nih.gov/31756345/.

Ahmed, S A, B D Hissong, D Verthelyi, K Donner, K Becker, and E Karpuzoglu-Sahin. 1999. "Gender and Risk of Autoimmune Diseases: Possible Role of Estrogenic Compounds." U.S. National Library of Medicine. National Center for Biotechnology Information. https://pubmed.ncbi.nlm.nih.gov/10502531/.

Akers, Whitney. 2018. "Does a Uterus Really Double in Size During Menstruation?" Healthline. Healthline News. https://www.healthline.com/health-news/does-uterus-double-in-size-during-menstuation.

Andrew Weil Center for Integrative Medicine. 2020. Body of Wonder. Podcast audio. https://open.spotify.com/show/1YXvEnC68HMiPCt4tm4CDC?si=_-2rtgNxRimjfHdhMcM_Dg.

Antwis, Rachael E, Katie L Edwards, Bryony Unwin, Susan L Walker, and Susanne Shultz. 2019. "Rare Gut Microbiota Associated with Breeding Success, Hormone Metabolites and Ovarian Cycle Phase in the Critically Endangered Eastern Black Rhino." US National Library of Medicine. National Institutes of Health. https://www.ncbi.nlm.nih.gov/pmc/articles/PMC6377766/.

Apel, Molly. 2020. "Does Your Gut Control Your Immune System? The Science behind the Connection." Bulletproof. Emily Gonzalez, ND. https://www.bulletproof.com/gut-health/immune-system-in-gut.

Asprey, Dave. 2020a. Interview with Dr. Kari Nadeau. "#768: New Solutions for the Growing Allergy Epidemic" in The Human Upgrade. Spotify, 01:11:00. https://open.spotify.com/episode/1WJxBuofK1XUBP91YYL1T1?si=b38c7646ae684356.

Asprey, Dave. 2020b. Interview with Sarah Hill, Ph.D. "#665: The Birth Control Episode: The Pill Isn't Bulletproof" in The Human Upgrade. Spotify, 01:23:00. https://open.spotify.com/episode/1p2j6kZDyrKTZ4FLU196fF?si=393d818a23814887.

Baker, Fiona C, and Helen S Driver. 2007. "Circadian Rhythms, Sleep, and the Menstrual Cycle." U.S. National Library of Medicine. National Center for Biotechnology Information. https://www.ncbi.nlm.nih.gov/pubmed/17383933.

Barrington, Meghan, and Aleena Kanner. 2019. Move Your Brain Move Your Body. Podcast audio. https://open.spotify.com/

show/6eUH3hUwMRci806Y8V23L2?si=svosL5MiTXCrECNx_ HWoCA.

Bedosky, Lauren. 2018. "Do I Need More Calories During My Period?" LIVESTRONG. https://www.livestrong.com/article/441187-do-i-need-more-calories-during-my-period/.

Bennett, Dr. Sarah. 2019. "What Is Cortisol? Why Does It Matter? Everything You Need to Know." Natural Med Doc. https://naturalmeddoc.com/blog/cortisol/.

Bergen, Robert. 2021. "Low Testosterone in Women: Causes, Symptoms, and Treatments." Farr Institute. https://www.farrinstitute.org/low-testosterone-in-women.

Boutot, Maegan. 2018. "The Immune System and the Menstrual Cycle." Clue. https://helloclue.com/articles/cycle-a-z/the-immune-system-and-the-menstrual-cycle.

Brainum, Jerry. 2013. "Muscle Growth and Estrogen." Iron Man Magazine. Hormones. https://www.ironmanmagazine.com/muscle-growth-and-estrogen/.

Brown, Brene. 2015. Daring Greatly: How the Courage to Be Vulnerable Transforms the Way We Live, Love, Parent, and Lead. United States: Penguin Publishing Group.

Byrne, Andrew. 2020. The Singing Athlete: Brain-Based Training for Your Voice. United States: Andrew Byrne Studio Incorporated.

Calderone, Karen L. 1990. "The Infulence of Gender on the Frequency of Pain and Sedative Medication Administered to Postoperative Patients." SpringerLink. Kluwer Academic Publishers-Plenum Publishers. https://link.springer.com/article/10.1007/BF00289259.

Chavarro, Jorege E, Janet W Rich-Edwards, Bernard A Rosner, and Walter C Willett. 2011. "A Prospective Study of Dietary Carbohydrate Quantity and Quality in Relation to Risk of Ovulatory Infection." U.S. National Library of Medicine. National Institutes of Health. https://www.ncbi.nlm.nih.gov/pmc/articles/PMC3066074/.

Chidi-Ogbolu, Nkechinyere, and Keith Baar. 2019. "Effect of Estrogen on Musculoskeletal Performance and Injury Risk." Frontiers in Physiology. REVIEW. https://www.frontiersin.org/articles/10.3389/fphys.2018.01834/full.

Cohen, I T, B B Sherwin, and A S Fleming. 1987. "Food Cravings, Mood, and the Menstrual Cycle." U.S. National Library of Medicine. National Center for Biotechnology. https://www.ncbi.nlm.nih.gov/pubmed/3428887.

"Contraceptive Use." 2020. Centers for Disease Control and Prevention. National Center for Healthy Statistics. https://www.cdc.gov/nchs/fastats/contraceptive.htm.

"Cortisol." 2021. Menopause Woman. https://www.menopausewoman.com/hormones/cortisol/.

"COVID-19 Vaccination Associated With a Small, Temporary Increase in Menstrual Cycle Length, Suggests NIH-Funded Study." 2022. National Institutes of Health. U.S. Department of Health and Human Services. https://www.nih.gov/news-events/news-releases/covid-19-vaccination-associated-small-temporary-increase-menstrual-cycle-length-suggests-nih-funded-study.

D'Eon, Tara, and Barry Braun. 2002. "The Roles of Estrogen and Progesterone in Regulating Carbohydrate and Fat Utilization at Rest and During Exercise." U.S. National Library of Medicine. National Center for Biotechnology Information. https://www.ncbi.nlm.nih.gov/pubmed/11988133.

Doyle, Glennon. 2020. Untamed. United States: Random House Publishing Group.

Dusenbery, Maya. 2018. Doing Harm: The Truth About How Bad Medicine and Lazy Science Leave Women Dismissed, Misdiagnosed, and Sick. United States: HarperOne.

Escalante Pulido, J M, and M Alpizar Salazar. 1999. "Changes in Insulin Sensitivity, Secretion and Glucose Effectiveness During Menstrual Cycle." U.S. National Library of Medicine. National Center for Biotechnology Information. https://www.ncbi.nlm.nih.gov/pubmed/10071420.

Fairweather, DeLisa, and Noel R. Rose. 2004. "Women and Autoimmune Diseases." Centers for Disease Control and Prevention. Emerging Infectious Diseases. https://wwwnc.cdc.gov/eid/article/10/11/04-0367_article.

"Female Fat Loss Guide - Understanding the Menstrual Cycle and Your Fat Loss Goals." 2019. Performance Project. https://www.performanceproject.co.uk/understanding-menstrual-cycle-fat-loss-goals-2/.

Fields, Helen. 2015. "The Gut: Where Bacteria and Immune System Meet." Johns Hopkins Medicine. https://www.hopkinsmedicine.org/research/advancements-in-research/fundamentals/in-depth/the-gut-where-bacteria-and-immune-system-meet.

Fogel, Alan. 2012. "Emotional and Physical Pain Activate Similar Brain

Regions: Where does emotion hurt in the body?" Psychology Today. https://www.psychologytoday.com/intl/blog/body-sense/201204/emotional-and-physical-pain-activate-similar-brain-regions.

Hadjistavropoulos, Thomas, Bruce McMurtry, and Kenneth D Craig. 2007. "Beautiful Faces in Pain: Biases and Accuracy in the Perception of Pain." Taylor & Francis Online. Psychology & Health. https://www.tandfonline.com/doi/abs/10.1080/08870449608400268.

Hamidovic, Ajna, Kristina Karapetyan, Fadila Serdarevic, So Hee Choi, Tory Eisenlohr-Moul, and Graziano Pinna. 2020. "Higher Circulating Cortisol in the Follicular vs. Luteal Phase of the Menstrual Cycle: A Meta-Analysis." Frontiers in Endocrinology. Neuroendocrine Science. https://www.frontiersin.org/articles/10.3389/fendo.2020.00311/full.

Hill, Maisie. 2019. Period Power: Harness Your Hormones and Get Your Cycle Working For You. United Kingdom: Bloomsbury USA.

Hill, Maisie. 2020. Period Power. Podcast audio. https://open.spotify.com/show/1FxxjMAYrSncVYhJwYsFja?si=fUsXkIqrRd-SwIPFQOSANQ.

Hill, Sarah. 2019. This Is Your Brain on Birth Control: The Surprising Science of Women, Hormones, and the Law of Unintended Consequences. United States: Penguin Publishing Group.

Hoffman, Diane E, and Anita J Tarzian. 2001. "The Girl Who Cried Pain: A Bias Against Women in the Treatment of Pain." Digital Commons at UM Carey Law. University of Maryland Francis King Carey School of Law. https://digitalcommons.law.umaryland.edu/cgi/viewcontent.cgi?article=1144&context=fac_pubs.

Hoffman, Kelly M, Sophie Trawalter, Jordan R Axt, and M. Norman Oliver. 2016. "Racial Bias in Pain Assessment and Treatment Recommendations, and False Beliefs About Biological Differences Between Blacks and Whites." Edited by Susan T Fiske. PNAS. National Academy of Sciences. https://www.pnas.org/content/113/16/4296.

Horton, Dr. Jodi. 2021. "Everything You Need to Know about Condoms." The Love Club. https://club.lovewellness.com/post/everything-you-need-to-know-about-condoms-6022cb619c285c4069506d63.

Hurn, Patricia D, and Lawrence M Brass. 2003. "Estrogen and Stroke: A Balanced Analysis." Stroke. https://www.ahajournals.org/doi/full/10.1161/01.STR.0000054051.88378.25.

Janse DE Jonge, Xanne A K, Martin W Thompson, Vivienne H Chuter, Leslie N Silk, and Jeanette M Thom. 2012. "Exercise Performance Over the Menstrual Cycle in Temperate and Hot, Humid Conditions."

U.S. National Library of Medicine. National Center for Biotechnology Information. https://www.ncbi.nlm.nih.gov/pubmed/22776870.

Jardim, Nicole. 2018. "PP# 83: Your Gut Microbiome & Your Vaginal Health with Kiran Krishnan," in The Period Party Podcast, Spotify, 36:45, https://open.spotify.com/episode/7GYsyu4RjTPUE98Vqjsh2i?si=c959836066674a5d.

Jardim, Nicole. 2016. The Period Party Podcast. https://open.spotify.com/show/0yMPEV8aehFkMcODYRUqtO?si=V5vPdfF9SLiGyjaPG5rKYA.

Jardim, Nicole. 2021. "When It's Not Just Endo - The Connection Between SIBO, IBS, IC and Endometriosis with Jessica Duffin." The Period Party Podcast. https://open.spotify.com/episode/6eHJh4IW94WqndAE09QakR?si=Syj4Mx26R-G9_J-yhUvN-A.

Jennings, Rebecca. 2017. "Performance Nutrition During the Menstrual Cycle." Nutritionist Resource. Women's Nutrition. https://www.nutritionist-resource.org.uk/memberarticles/performance-nutrition-during-the-menstrual-cycle.

Kahler, Dr. Antonella. 2020. "The Progesterone Paradox: How Hormones Can Affect Women's Training." Muscle & Strength. https://www.muscleandstrength.com/articles/the-progesterone-paradox.

Kiesel, Laura. 2017. "Women and Pain: Disparities in Experience and Treatment." Harvard Health Publishing. Harvard Medical School. https://www.health.harvard.edu/blog/women-and-pain-disparities-in-experience-and-treatment-2017100912562.

Kindelan, Katie. 2019. "USWNT Used Innovative Period Tracking to Help Player Performance at World Cup." Good Morning America. https://www.goodmorningamerica.com/wellness/story/uswnt-innovative-period-tracking-player-performance-world-cup-64339368.

Knight, Chris. 1995. Blood Relations: Menstruation and the Origins of Culture. United Kingdom: Yale University Press.

Kristiansen, Trine. 2019. "How Stress Affects the Luteal Phase and the Production of Progesterone." TRINE KRISTIANSEN. https://www.trinekristiansen.no/lognew-blog/2019/2/25/how-stress-affects-the-luteal-phase-and-the-production-of-progesterone.

Leblanc, D.R., M. Schneider, P. Angele, G. Vollmer, and D. Docheva. 2017. "The Effect of Estrogen on Tendon and Ligament Metabolism and Function." Science Direct. The Journal of Steroid Biochemistry and Molecular Biology. https://www.sciencedirect.com/science/article/pii/S0960076017301590.

Levin, V A, X Jiang, and R Kagan. 2018. "Estrogen Therapy for

Osteoporosis in the Modern Era." U.S. National Library of Medicine. National Center for Biotechnology Information. https://pubmed.ncbi.nlm.nih.gov/29520604/.

Levine, Beth. "Autoimmunity Rates Are on the Rise in the United States, Study Says." EverydayHealth, April 17, 2020. https://www.everydayhealth.com/autoimmune-diseases/autoimmunity-rates-on-the-rise-in-the-united-states-study-says/.

Lin, Steven. 2019. The Dental Diet: The Surprising Link Between Your Teeth, Real Food, and Life-Changing Natural Health. United States: Hay House.

Liu, Katherine A, and Natalie A Dipietro Mager. 2016. "Women's Involvement in Clinical Trials: Historical Perspective and Future Implications." US National Library of Medicine. National Institutes of Health. https://www.ncbi.nlm.nih.gov/pmc/articles/PMC4800017/.

Mintz, Laurie. 2015. "The Orgasm Gap: Simple Truth & Sexual Solutions." Psychology Today. https://www.psychologytoday.com/us/blog/stress-and-sex/201510/the-orgasm-gap-simple-truth-sexual-solutions.

Montero-Lopez, Eva, Ana Santos-Ruiz, M. Carmen Garcia-Rios, Manuel Rodriguez-Blazquez, Heather L. Rogers, and Maria Isabel Peralta-Ramirez. 2018. "The Relationship Between the Menstrual Cycle and Cortisol Secretion: Daily and Stress-Invoked Cortisol Patterns." Science Direct. International Journal of Psychophysiology. https://www.sciencedirect.com/science/article/abs/pii/S0167876017302696.

Nestor, James.2020. Breath: The New Science of a Lost Art. United States: Penguin Publishing Group.

O'Bryan, Tom. 2016. The Autoimmune Fix: How to Stop the Hidden Autoimmune Damage That Keeps You Sick, Fat, and Tired Before It Turns Into Disease. United States: Rodale Books.

Osborn, Corinne O'Keefe. 2018. "Anti-Androgen: Uses for Men and Women, Types, and Side Effects." Healthline. Healthline Media. https://www.healthline.com/health/anti-androgen#side-effects.

"Paula Radcliffe: Sport Has Not Learned About Periods." 2015. Web Interview. BBC Sport. https://www.bbc.com/sport/athletics/30927245.

Peach, Lucy. 2020. Period Queen: Life hack your cycle and own your power all month long. Australia: Allen & Unwin.

"Premenstrual Dysphoric Disorder (PMDD)." Accessed 2021. Johns Hopkins Medicine. https://www.hopkinsmedicine.org/health/conditions-and-diseases/premenstrual-dysphoric-disorder-pmdd.

Raimi, Sam, dir. 2002. Spider-man. Culver City, California: Columbia TriStar Home Entertainment. Film, 121 minutes.
Reed, Beverly G, and Bruce R Carr. 2018. "The Normal Menstrual Cycle and the Control of Ovulation." National Center for Biotechnology Information. U.S. National Library of Medicine. https://www.ncbi.nlm.nih.gov/books/NBK279054/.
Sairs, Rebecca. 2020. Power Over PMDD.
    Podcast audio. https://open.spotify.com/show/3lUKWna4veCTC8t94lfO6P?si=RSd5NzQpRwqxPnr1PATSEw.
Scott, Jennifer Acosta. 2012. "How Your Menstrual Cycle Affects Your Behavior." Edited by Lindsey Marcellin. EverydayHealth. https://www.everydayhealth.com/womens-health/how-your-menstrual-cycle-affects-your-behavior.aspx.
Sims, Stacy, and Selene Yeager. 2016. ROAR: How to Match Your Food and Fitness to Your Unique Female Physiology for Optimum Performance, Great Health, and a Strong, Lean Body for Life. United States: Rodale Books.
Smith, Bren. 2019. Eat Like a Fish: My Adventures as a Fisherman Turned Restorative Ocean Farmer. United States: Alfred A. Knopf.
Solomon, S. J., M. S. Kurzer, and D. H. Calloway. 1982. "Menstrual Cycle and Basal Metabolic Rate in Women." Experts@Minnesota. University of Minnesota. https://experts.umn.edu/en/publications/menstrual-cycle-and-basal-metabolic-rate-in-women.
Spheeris, Penelope, dir. 1994. The Little Rascals. Amblin Entertainment. Film, 82 minutes.
Steilen-Matias, Danielle R. Accessed 2021. "Oral Contraceptive Use | Does Estrogen Cause or Prevent ACL Injury?" Caring Medical. https://www.caringmedical.com/prolotherapy-news/estrogen-ligament-laxity/.
Tunks, Eldon, Anthony Bellissimo, and Ranjan Roy. 1990. "Chronic Pain: Psychosocial Factors in Rehabilitation, 2nd Edition." APA PsychNet. American Psychological Association. https://psycnet.apa.org/record/1990-98104-000.
Unger, Cecile A. 2016. "Hormone Therapy for Transgender Patients." US National Library of Medicine. National Institutes of Health. https://www.ncbi.nlm.nih.gov/pmc/articles/PMC5182227/.
Vitti, Alisa. 2013. WomanCode: Perfect Your Cycle, Amplify Your Fertility, Supercharge Your Sex Drive, and Become a Power Source. United Kingdom: Hay House.

Vitti, Alisa. 2019. "Period Blood - What the Colour of Your Period Blood Can Tell You about Your Health and Fertility." FLO Living. https://www.floliving.com/the-color-of-your-period-blood-2/.

Vitti, Alisa. 2020. In the FLO: Unlock Your Hormonal Advantage and Revolutionize Your Life. United Kingdom: HarperOne.

Wambach, Abby. 2019. WOLFPACK: How to Come Together, Unleash Our Power, and Change the Game. United States: Celadon Books.

Wu, Jianhua, Chris P Gale, Marlous Hall, Tatendashe B Dondo, Elizabeth Metcalfe, Ged Oliver, Phil D Batin, Harry Hemingway, Adam Timmis, and Robert M West. 2016. "Impact of Initial Hospital Diagnosis on Mortality for Acute Myocardial Infarction: A National Cohort Study." SAGE Journals. https://journals.sagepub.com/doi/full/10.1177/2048872616661693.

"Your Menstrual Cycle." 2018. Office on Women's Health. https://www.womenshealth.gov/menstrual-cycle/your-menstrual-cycle.

Zhang, Lanlan, Elizabeth A Reynolds Losin, Yoni K Ashar, Leonie Koban, and Tor D Wager. 2021. "Gender Biases in Estimation of Others' Pain." ScienceDirect. The Journal of Pain. https://www.sciencedirect.com/science/article/pii/S1526590021000353?dgcid=raven_sd_aip_email.

UNLEASH YOUR S⚕PERPOWERS

Korra O'Neill, otherwise known as Coach Korra, is an integrative nutrition health coach and future JD-holder out of New York. Her fascination with our human hardware started when she was small and has grown into an insatiable curiosity regarding how we can utilize body acceptance as a tool for wellbeing for the entirety of humankind. When she isn't studying for law school, listening to experts discuss their research, or reading books by activists and thought-leaders, she can be found binge watching superhero shows or putzing around her house while belting to the same three songs on repeat. Korra is a vocal member of both the queer and neurodivergent communities and hopes this book can help spread their common message that: not only is everybody different, but that difference is what makes us each spectacularly glorious.

UNLEASH YOUR S⚢PERPOWERS

    Tara Lynn Steele, otherwise known as Coach TL, is a functional range conditioning (mobility) specialist and future MBA holder. Her curiosity carried her on a path filled with creativity, body awareness, and wiggles! Human hardware and its intricacies are her everyday. When she's not writing this book, taking MBA classes, or training clients, she can be found hanging upside down on an aerial apparatus, exploring nature through hiking or camping, teaching dance, or working on the latest choreography spinning in her head. TL is a lover of animals and sustainability--she votes with her dollar, supports underrepresented groups, and is keen on the idea that communication is key. Her favorite language is that of the body and hopes to spread the word of love and acceptance to all bodies.

About the Authors

CPSIA information can be obtained
at www.ICGtesting.com
Printed in the USA
LVHW020935080622
720761LV00010B/799